Teaching Civics in Unstable Times

Teaching Civics in Unstable Times

Guidelines for Defining "We" in American Democracy

Andrew Tripodo

ROWMAN & LITTLEFIELD
Lanham • Boulder • New York • London

Published by Rowman & Littlefield
An imprint of The Rowman & Littlefield Publishing Group, Inc.
4501 Forbes Boulevard, Suite 200, Lanham, Maryland 20706
www.rowman.com

6 Tinworth Street, London SE11 5AL, United Kingdom

British Library Cataloguing in Publication Information Available

Library of Congress Cataloging-in-Publication Data

Names: Tripodo, Andrew, 1989- author.
Title: Teaching civics in unstable times : guidelines for defining "we" in American democracy / Andrew Tripodo.
Description: Lanham, Maryland : Rowman & Littlefield, 2022. | Includes bibliographical references. | Summary: "Civic educators need new strategies to prepare young people for democratic citizenship. Complete with student-facing lesson plans that can be modified for any age, Teaching Civics in Unstable Times offers three rules for creating classrooms that prepare young people to be engaged contributors to their local, regional, and national communities"—Provided by publisher.
Identifiers: LCCN 2021021624 (print) | LCCN 2021021625 (ebook) | ISBN 9781475856088 (cloth) | ISBN 9781475856095 (paperback) | ISBN 9781475856101 (epub)
Subjects: LCSH: Civics—Study and teaching—United States. | Community and school—United States.
Classification: LCC LC1091 .T537 2022 (print) | LCC LC1091 (ebook) | DDC 370.11/5—dc23
LC record available at https://lccn.loc.gov/2021021624
LC ebook record available at https://lccn.loc.gov/2021021625

To the memory of Mary Ellen O'Brien, the most inspired wordsmith and loving teacher I've ever known.

Contents

Preface

"Democracy," I tell my students, "is the simple and radical idea that 50 percent + 1 (a majority) of citizens should control the state." Rather than leaving statecraft to highly educated elites, democracies make all citizens members of the ruling class. In so doing, they create an immense need for widely distributed, high-quality education in democratic leadership. In the United States, this type of education is encapsulated by the term "civics," and is in grave need of reform.

Remarkably, democracy's central premise—that the majority of citizens should control public policy—has become the legitimizing principle for power across the globe today. Countries with long histories of elaborate and deep social hierarchy (like Spain) have baked the egalitarian principles of popular government into the foundations of their society, and clearly authoritarian nations (like Russia) go through the trouble of putting on sham elections. That illiberal leaders in nations like Russia feel the need to ape majority rule to hold onto power demonstrates the triumph of the democratic ideal: closed door government controlled exclusively by elites unaccountable to their people are seen as illegitimate.

But making governors of citizens requires more than a formal change in status—citizens also have to think and act like leaders of a huge collective project. Whereas monarchies and oligarchies need only educate their chosen sons in the art of statecraft, democracies depend on an educated and wise citizenry. Preparing an entire citizenry for collective leadership is no easy task, and we—as a nation and globe—

are failing. Researchers from the University of Cambridge and Pew have recorded democratic discontent (that is, dissatisfaction with democratic government) to be at global twenty-five-year highs. And democracy's global march has slowed and actually reversed in recent years, with 2020 being the first year in decades when non-democracies outnumbered democracies globally.

In other words, people are generally unsatisfied with their own work as collective governors, and are gravitating toward authoritative leaders who can offer simple, forceful solutions to subtle, complex problems. I will argue that poor civic education is the cause of this national and global low-water line for democracy, and that revitalized civic education is the solution.

AMERICAN FOUNDING DOCUMENTS: USER MANUALS FOR CITIZENS

The majorities that govern democracies are neither inherently wise nor especially efficient—in fact, they can be just as tyrannical, prejudiced, and stupid as single individuals. When the general population is not capable of seriously deliberating about the shared fate of our nation, when they lack the skills and mental habits of leaders, democracies can become chaotic and unresponsive, leading to a political culture defined by cynicism and close-minded tribalism.

History furnishes far more examples of democracies crumbling from the inside than being conquered by foreign enemies—since they rely on the leadership and cooperation of so many, democracies are risky endeavors. Some democracies (like the US so far) have limited these risks by instilling democratic ethics into their citizens—a basic set of values that tell us how to treat one another in the political arena. Our nation's founding documents are our first teachers of these values, and our schools must use these documents to become the second. Founding documents act as user manuals for citizens seeking to use their political powers for good and as rubric against which to assess the justness of actions by the majority.

To help citizens govern, the US Constitution sets parameters on the public will, and channels it in ways that will reduce its potential for harm. The Bill of Rights protects the rights of minorities against the potential "tyranny of the majority," and the Federalist Papers and Declaration of Independence describe the relationship between Americans and their government. These documents are meant to teach the values that American citizens—as self-governors—must embody as we go through the messy and hard work of steering this diverse and huge nation together.

Behind the eighteenth-century conceits and institutional structures, American founding documents profess a set of values that translate into a culture and way of life that citizen self-governors must embody if we hope to rule with wisdom. The most important role of civics educators is to help students understand these essentially American and essentially democratic values, and live this way of life.

This book will offer an account of what it means to be an American citizen who is grounded in the values taught in our nation's foundational documents, and then offer concrete recommendations (and lesson plans) for civic educators seeking to help young people learn what it means to lead a democratic way of life.

AMERICAN DEMOCRATIC DECLINE AND CIVIC EDUCATION

American democracy degrades into populism when citizens come to closely identify with part of their nation instead of the whole of it. When we identify with particular ideologies more deeply than national democratic values, we endanger setting fire to the very arena that allows us to debate those ideologies in the first place. For democracies to be both inclusive and competent, representatives and citizens must practice civic virtue, which is a set of rules for getting along with people with whom our lives are intertwined and with whom we disagree.

In this country—where a lot of people depend on each other and frequently disagree—practicing civic virtue means maintaining an open mind, seeking common ground, fighting in good faith for your beliefs, and never allowing disagreement to devolve into violence. Our government structures were designed for people who practice these virtues, and they don't work properly when we don't. For our representatives to abandon the type of scorched earth politics that hobble government effectiveness and engender a culture of cynicism, *voters* must expect them to do so and punish them at the ballot box when they don't.

The freedom and prosperity that has defined American life in the modern era hinges on our collective ability to be at once proud individuals who are willing and able to passionately advocate for their interests and considerate members of a larger, self-governing community that frequently disagrees on what is best. This is no easy task, and certainly not one for which any of us is born ready. In fact—as Jonathan Haidt persuasively argues in *The Righteous Mind*—our psychology encourages us to do the opposite. When faced with conflict, we are hard-wired to reflexively dig in our heels and side with our in-group. And that's what Americans have tended to do.

Haidt's research points to truth that democracies do not spring naturally from the human heart. They need to be deliberately created and actively maintained, and at their hearts are shared values that insist on individual dignity, basic equality, and personal agency. New generations need to be molded into democratic citizens, lest we risk their natural impulses carrying them toward lives defined by public indifference or partisan fury.

In their important book *Upswing*, political scientists Robert Putnam and Shaylyn Romney Garrett compare the United States today to the fraught Gilded Age at the end of the nineteenth century, when profound political polarization, extreme economic inequality, and widespread mistrust between Americans made solving national problems—no matter how deeply and widely felt—nearly impossible. They go on to document how we escaped that dark nadir and went on to experience roughly eighty years of ever-growing cross-party collaboration, economic equality, and neighborly goodwill. That trend reversed sometime in the 1970s, and has moved down ever since, leaving us nearly as politically polarized, economically unequal, and distrustful of one another as we were 125 years ago.

Putnam and Garrett attribute no discrete cause to the upswing that defined the first half of the twentieth century and then the reversal that has continued until today (and accelerated in recent years), and neither can I. Discerning causality in the social sciences is a perennial challenge, as inputs (such as the behavior of politicians, the media landscape, grassroots activism, and dozens more) are deeply intertwined and self-reinforcing. We cannot in good faith tease out any one cause that explains the hostile and fragmented political milieu that currently defines American political life. Certainly, divisive political leaders and a fractured media environment play a part, as do low rates of membership in civic associations. But no one event or trend fully accounts for the general alienation Americans feel from our governing institutions and each other.

I will argue that schools, as the culture-making institutions with the farthest reach in American life, play an essential role in rehabilitating our national dialogue and restoring our ability to function as an inclusive democracy that is responsive to the needs of all its people. It's up to schools to help young people define the "we" in American democracy—to explore what we as citizens owe one another, and what values to hold ourselves to.

The claim that a failure of civic education is at the heart of our national troubles is not new, and has indeed become such a reflexive response to political antagonism that some scholars have begun to wonder whether we're asking too much of US history and government teachers. In a thoughtful piece titled "What the Capitol riot means for civics education," the Fordham Institute's Dale Chu writes:

> The rabble that ransacked the Capitol probably wouldn't have changed if they had been better versed in the theory behind America's founding. But from an education standpoint, they might not have become so strident if they hadn't been so vulnerable to brainwashing in the first place—a vulnerability that could have been inoculated against in school as part of a curriculum that trains students to think critically and instills a respect, even a reverence, for knowledge and evidence.

In other words, Chu believes that the pervasive hostility that is eating our politics goes deeper than civics and social studies, and that reversing it will require a broader reassessment of the goals of American education. Chu is right to believe that a stronger understanding of the three branches of government and purpose of the Declaration of Independence probably wouldn't have altered the rioter's actions, but his assessment reveals an overly narrow understanding of what "civics education" means.

The goal of civics education isn't merely to communicate a body of knowledge, it's to prepare young people for the trials of self-government—a task for which knowledge is necessary but not sufficient. More than merely understanding our governing institutions and founding documents, self-governors must be able to channel the values contained in those documents into public life. To effectively use America's democratic institutions, citizens need to be able to communicate their vision for the country, listen to the contrasting visions of others with an open mind, and clarify differences while seeking common ground. They must, in other words, translate American principles and institutional processes into *a way of life* that is defined by mutual reciprocity and evidence-driven debate, tolerance of differences, and grace in victory and defeat.

To avoid the trap of viewing America politics as an all out war (one that is ultimately self-defeating regardless of your side), young Americans must learn to see themselves as part of a truly national project, not a merely regional or tribal one.

If our schools had prioritized civic education when the rioters were young, perhaps they would have recognized that the forum for contesting the results of American elections are the courts, that patriots support the peaceful transition of power even when they don't support the winning candidate, and that the America that they hold dear was forged in the fire of logical, sometimes vitriolic, but always peaceful, debate. Civic education should produce Americans who rely on reason and evidence more than statements from their leaders, and teach them that our democratic institutions and processes (like the process by which a new president is determined) must be defended even when their leaders seek to undermine them. In short, Mr. Chu is right about how education can help us recover from our charged politics, but he's wrong to think that the solution is outside the scope of civics.

For better or for worse, our political culture runs through our classrooms. This book is about those classrooms.

Introduction

This book offers an expansive view of civic education that recognizes the central role that widely and deeply held democratic values play in a functional, tolerant, diverse, and large democracy. It calls on administrators, curriculum writers, professors of education, and, most importantly, K–12 teachers, to champion civics as more than a set of facts, but as a way of life, and proposes a set of strategies for doing so. These rules are meant to offer a new way for educators to conceive of civic education, one that will help us more successfully approach the monumental task of preparing future generations for collective governance.

Part I proposes three new strategies for teaching civic content that highlights the essential role that young people play in any dynamic and successful democracy. Each strategy has the goal of helping young people build a relationship with our country that is optimistic, clear-eyed, and reciprocal. They are strategies that emphasize the collective nature of citizenship, and the necessity of participation in the national project. Chapters include lesson plans, which are inconsistently formatted by design and intended to showcase an array of instructional strategies. They are meant to be modified by teachers according to grade and period length. All lesson plans are student-facing.

Part II hones in on the habits that define democratic citizenship, habits that must be explicitly taught if they are to stick and habits that have been largely ignored in American classrooms for decades. Part III offers advice for school and district leaders interested in democratizing their school's structures to increase student participation and invest-ment in their school community.

This book argues that political culture runs through civics class-rooms, and offers arguments, strategies, and lesson plans to help educa-tors prepare our young people to lead this ever-flawed, but ever "more perfect" union toward a future that is more prosperous, just, and in-spired.

Part I

New Instructional Strategies for Government, Economics, and US History

Chapter One

Rule #1

Teach Debate as a Core American Value

AMERICAN CITIZENSHIP IS DEFINED BY CONTINUOUS DEBATE—LET'S PRESENT IT AS SUCH

What we now deem to be orthodox K–12 curriculum in American history, government, and economics were born from the fires of fierce debate and continue to be defined by principles that are deeply unharmonious. To honor the ongoing debates at the heart of American social science and politics, educators must consider and present them as subjects in flux, open questions in need of further consideration and new ideas, not dusty realms of settled information meant to be uncritically memorized.

US history, government, economics, and civics are disciplines that have been perennially refined by scholars, activists, and educators alike, but ultimately, it's the next generation that must accept and embody any philosophy of America. In doing so, that generation takes their place at the helm of the country. Educators must involve their students in the study of this country, not merely dictate the (contested) understandings of it.

THE WAR OVER THE MEANING OF OUR PAST:
DEBATE IN US HISTORY

The lessons to be learned from American history have never been decided, and the question of who deserves to be an authority on our history remains open. Given the fundamental disagreements over what and how to teach our young people about American History, many educators have elected to offer controversy-free "objective" accounts of America's past. But is this truly possible? Does the United States have a neutral history to tell? Unlike many questions about our nation's past, this question can be answered briefly and completely: no.

History cannot be an unedited onslaught of unfiltered facts—there are simply too many facts and (for most of us) too little time. Attempts at an "objective" teaching of US history—one free from ideology and personal bias—can only happen if we offer a truly exhaustive account of all of the events since the founding of our nation, without comment or commentary. Such a strategy is exhausting, unengaging, and logistically untenable.

To teach US history, we need to decide what to cut from it and what to emphasize, and those decisions require value judgments. What is "relevant" to the Italian immigrant may not be to the Native American. The moment we begin the necessary process of editing history for a classroom, bias seeps in. There has never been a bias-free US history class and there probably never will be. In this sense, K–12 US history is political, since what we teach young people is an unavoidably partial account of our nation that will nevertheless influence their relationship with it for the rest of their lives.

WHAT MUST AMERICANS KNOW ABOUT OUR NATION?

Every social studies educator, whether they create state testing standards, write curriculum, or teach students directly, begins their planning process with the (conscious or unconscious) question: "What must Americans know about our nation?" The truth is there is no answer to that question that is not informed by personal beliefs and political ideologies. For many years, but never more potently than today, the answer has been a storm of discordance.

Historians, educators, activists, and prominent politicians disagree vehemently about what young people should know about the American project. For example: to what extent did the obvious (and at the time socially expected) sexism and racism of our founding fathers undermine the egalitarian principles they penned when declaring our independence? How we answer that question will determine whether we emphasize Enlightenment philosophy's influence on our national morality or instead focus on the moral hypocrisy of our founding. We can (and should) do both, but with limited time, what should we *emphasize*?

With limited time, should teachers walk students through the complexities of the Native American cultures that were all but wiped out by Europeans? Or should we spend more time teaching students about the culture and mannerisms of our English conquerors (should we call them conquerors, or explorers?)? Both topics are valuable, but where to linger? Where to invest valuable class time?

Educators can and must decide which American origin story to believe, and we have to decide for ourselves whether to view our founders as geniuses or hypocrites, but we can't decide that for our students. Every event in American history offers an array of interpretive options, each one setting us up for a different type of relationship with the American present. Faced with debate about the meaning of nearly all of those events, we can't choose sides and declare ourselves narrators of just one interpretation of our nation's history.

Instead, we must help our students participate in this never-ending great debate by offering a multitude of interpretive lenses. There is no one American story, and it's irresponsible and arrogant for those of us who work in civics education to pretend that there is. Skilled historians and virtuous democratic citizens share a common trait: they're curious rather than hostile when presented with new information and continuously seek to refine their worldviews through inquiry.

Our nation has always been defined by debate. And more important than young Americans learning the outcome of the War of 1812 is that they learn to integrate the capacity for open-minded, congenial, rigorous disagreement into their identities. US history teachers can help our nation recover from this period of social and political convulsion by helping young people integrate the national value of open debate into their understanding of who they are. Rather than choosing an ideological perch from which to teach US history, educators should teach their students to consider our history as one long, fierce, and unresolved debate, and embody that message by demonstrating stubborn open-mindedness ourselves.

Presenting American history in this way undercuts our own biases and ensures that we don't pass them down to our students. It also gives students a template for living the American ideal of constant intellectual exchange. As educators, we are not ideologues (as much as we may be in our private lives): it's our job to frame the debates about our history for students and help them understand the indispensable and defining place that open debate plays in our national identity (and the one that it should play in theirs too).

LESSON PLANS

US history classes must promote a culture of questioning, grounded in the recognition that history cannot be honestly told through one lens, in one way, and carry one unified series of lessons. It's complicated and ambiguous, and understanding it requires nuance, patience, and skepticism. The lessons we draw from our history must be considered by each individual, not dictated by a curriculum or instructor—it's the instructor's job to help students work through the complexities of our history to discern the lessons that make the most sense to them. The following lesson plans offer examples of how to teach this more open-ended version of American history, a version that emphasizes habits of inquiry over dead facts.

Below, I've listed lesson plans that have been successful in teaching fundamental topics of American history as engaging debates. They are meant to be student-facing. Please use them in full or approach them as starting places. They offer new ways of approaching essential topics in American history and effective strategies for engaging students. They are meant to be modified.

The lesson plans that appear throughout this book will vary in their level of detail and form. Some will offer minute-by-minute directions for students, some will simply introduce a topic and describe its relevance to a tenet of civic education, and most will fall somewhere in between. Some will open with open-ended questions for students to consider and some with a research assignment. Some will contain significant content and some will rely on teachers' ability to supply referenced content. I haven't found there to be any generalized lesson format that is manifestly superior to all others, and my intention is to offer educators a buffet of ways to approach lesson planning by showing examples of several different approaches.

Assignment #1: What Was the Meaning of the American Revolution? Our Founding Debate

TEXTBOX 1.1

Directions: Read the below introduction and answer the essential question at the bottom of the page. (You will have the opportunity to change your answer later.)

What did the American Revolution mean? What type of a republic did it establish? What principles did it champion? Whose interests did it further?

The American Revolution as a watershed moment in human history. The political philosophy that drove the revolution, and the governing documents that came out of it, were—compared to nearly every governing document before it—radically egalitarian. In their elegant assertion that governments exist to serve their people (and not the other way around), each of whom is born with sacred natural rights upon which no authority can infringe, they establish a framework for government that endows sovereignty and power onto common citizens and casts the state as a tool to be used by the people for their own benefit. This new governing philosophy was established in the shadow of global monarchy, which, for centuries had held the opposite view: that the ruling class were deserving of rights and privileges and the common people— entitled to little themselves—existed to serve them.

But the framers can also be understood less as enlightened statesmen and more as self-serving opportunists who succeeded in creating a government that used lofty rhetoric about equality and freedom to further their narrow interests.

As Thomas Jefferson penned the legendary phrase "All Men Are Created Equal," his slaves labored at home. The original US Constitution endowed only white male property owners with the power to vote, established a Senate that was not directly elected, and insisted on an Electoral College that would "refine and enlarge" the voices of the masses who cast their ballots for president. At the end of the day, the founders and people like them were the primary beneficiaries of the American Revolution and the form of government that it engendered.

Women, non-whites, and the poor gained little from the revolution, despite the rhetoric of equality and freedom. Focusing on the facts of early America rather than the rhetoric reveals a fundamentally racist, sexist, classist, and xenophobic nation cloaked in the principles of fairness, justice, and egalitarianism. Critical Consciousness Theory takes this line of analysis, and contends that the elevated values codified by our founders are rotted by a personal hypocrisy that still plagues our nation today.

- Essential Question: Was the founding of our nation the most successful egalitarian revolution in history, or a cynical power grab by landed white male gentry?

Part 1: Assignment

Directions:

1. Write a brief profile of ONE founding father using your textbook, outside sources, and other research materials (e.g., *Hamilton* the play).

    a. Where were they born? What was their childhood like?
    b. How did they get to the American colonies?
    c. What was their profession?
    d. Did they have slaves (indentured servants or African slaves)?
    e. What were their views on women?
    f. Why did they want to break away from Britain? Offer a brief explanation of their reasoning.

2. Share your profile with the class. Class takes notes on 3–5 founding fathers.
3. After hearing each summary, write down 2–3 adjectives that you think defines the person.
4. Share your adjectives with the class.
5. Based on your knowledge of the founding fathers, answer:

- Did they believe that *all people* are created equal? That every-one deserves the same basic rights?

Part 2: The Declaration of Independence

TEXTBOX 1.2

When in the Course of human events, it becomes necessary for one people to dissolve the political bands which have connected them with another, and to assume among the powers of the earth, the separate and equal station to which the Laws of Nature and of Nature's God entitle them, a decent respect to the opinions of mankind requires that they should declare the causes which impel them to the separation.

We hold these truths to be self-evident, that all men are creat-ed equal, that they are endowed by their Creator with certain unalienable Rights, that among these are Life, Liberty and the pursuit of Happiness.–That to secure these rights, Governments are instituted among Men, deriving their just powers from the consent of the governed, –That whenever any Form of Govern-ment becomes destructive of these ends, it is the Right of the People to alter or to abolish it, and to institute new Government, laying its foundation on such principles and organizing its powers in such form, as to them shall seem most likely to effect their Safety and Happiness. Prudence, indeed, will dictate that Govern-ments long established should not be changed for light and tran-sient causes; and accordingly all experience hath shewn, that mankind are more disposed to suffer, while evils are sufferable, than to right themselves by abolishing the forms to which they are accustomed. But when a long train of abuses and usurpations, pursuing invariably the same Object evinces a design to reduce them under absolute Despotism, it is their right, it is their duty, to throw off such Government, and to provide new Guards for their future security.–Such has been the patient sufferance of these Colonies; and such is now the necessity which constrains them to alter their former Systems of Government. The history of the present King of Great Britain is a history of repeated injuries and usurpations, all having in direct object the establishment of an absolute Tyranny over these States. To prove this, let Facts be submitted to a candid world.

1. Read the first two paragraphs of the Declaration of Independence (above) and summarize it in your own words.
2. What is the job of government? What qualities is every human endowed with?

Part 3: Debate

1. How did the actions and behaviors of the founding fathers differ from the values they penned in the Declaration of Independence?
2. Did the personal lives and beliefs of the founding fathers negate the values of equality and freedom upon which our nation is founded?
3. Essential Question: was the founding of our nation the most successful egalitarian revolution in history, or a cynical power grab by landed white male gentry?

Assignment #2: The Constitutional Convention: Equality Among States or People?

The drafting of the US Constitution was a raucous affair. While everyone agreed that the Articles of Confederation had failed, the Anti-Federalists came to the Constitutional Convention seeking modest amendments and the Federalists were set on a wholesale overhaul. At the heart of their disagreement was the question of state power—exactly how much power should states have to set their own agendas and disregard federal directives? Even more important is state representation within the federal government—would less populous states have the same power as highly populated ones in the Federal Legislative Branch, or would state influence in the Federal Legislature be tied to population?

Part 1: Think Like You're in New Jersey

- Half the Class: Imagine you lived in New Jersey (a very small, not very populous state) in 1788, when the structure of the Legislative Branch is being debated at the Constitutional Convention.
- Half the Class: Imagine you lived in Virginia (by far the most populous state) in 1788, when the structure of the Legislative Branch is being debated at the Constitutional Convention.
- Do you support the New Jersey Plan or the Virginia Plan? Explain your reasoning.

Part 2: Enlarge Your Perspective

Consider the perspective of the entire nation. Which system—the Virginia Plan or New Jersey Plan—seems most FAIR for all involved? Which plan will likely lead to a more representative republic (a republic in which everyone's voices are heard equally)?

- Make an argument for adopting EITHER the New Jersey Plan or the Virginia plan.

Part 3: Infer What Happened Based on the Legislative Branch of the United States

Read Article 1 of the US Constitution to answer: Who won the debate at the Constitutional Convention?

1. Does our Legislative Branch give states equal voting power, or do we give states with larger populations more representation in the federal government?
2. Did the proponents of the New Jersey Plan or Virginia Plan win the debate? Explain.

Part 4 (extension): Should We Pass a Constitutional Amendment that Eliminates the Senate? Use the Word "Sovereign" in Your Response

Some political scientists and activists lament the existence of the Senate, claiming that it distorts representation in this country. Because of the senate people living in low-population states have a disproportionate amount of representation in the federal government (and therefore the whole Congress).

But smaller states claim that eliminating the senate will essentially make them invisible to the federal government, since they will have insignificant voting power in the Legislative Branch. This lack of representation could lead to policies that harm them.

Take a stand: should we abolish the senate?

Assignment #3: Were the Doctrines of Manifest Destiny and the American Dream Justifiable? How Are the Two Concepts Related?

Part 1: What Was Manifest Destiny?

Figure 1.1 is a visual depiction of the doctrine of Manifest Destiny. Analyze the image, and then answer: what is the doctrine of Manifest Destiny?

Now that you know what it is, briefly consider: was the Doctrine of Manifest Destiny a positive development?

Part 2: Considering the Many Consequences of Manifest Destiny

Group Reading, Whole Class Share:
Directions:

1. Section ONE of the class: read excerpts on the innovations of the first Industrial Revolution that made westward expansion popular.

   a. Section TWO of the class: read excerpts on the Native American exploitation that took place during colonization.
   b. Section THREE of the class: read excerpts on the effect of westward expansion on white farmers and frontiersmen.

2. Summarize your readings to the class. Take notes on each others' summaries. You will need each perspective to render judgment on the doctrine of Manifest Destiny.
3. Answer: was Manifest Destiny justified? In your answer, be sure to consider WHO it benefitted and the assumptions upon which it was premised.

Figure 1.1. *American Progress*, chromolithograph print, c. 1873, after an 1872 painting of the same title by John Gast. *Library of Congress, Washington, D.C. (digital id: ppmsca 09855) https://www.britannica.com/event/ Manifest-Destiny#/media/1/362216/113284*

Part 3: Manifest Destiny and the American Dream

Do Now

You've heard of the American Dream (the term itself wasn't made popular until the 1930s, but it is used to describe the American experience from the beginning of our nation's founding until today).

1. What is the American Dream? What does it mean to you?
2. What emotions does the term evoke? As an American, how does it make you feel?

Do Now: Make the Connection

Which American founding document establishes the basis for the American Dream? Identify a founding document that lays out a philosophy that inspires and supports the American Dream and explain how it does so.

Do Now: Make the Next Connection

How is the American Dream related to Manifest Destiny? Think about the beliefs embedded in each.

Debate: Is the American Dream a Myth or Reality?

Assignment #4: Was the Civil War Preventable? Was There a Way to Abolish Slavery Without War?

Part 1: Identifying Specific Catalyzing Events

Since the moment of our founding, the institution of slavery threatened to tear us apart. Thomas Jefferson famously summed up the nation's position as "like holding a wolf by the ears, we can neither hold him nor safely let him go." As slavery became increasingly embedded into the economy and culture of the American South, making its abolition unthinkable to southern landowners and the political class, northern discomfort with the institution grew into full throated outrage. The dispute over slavery was the largest wedge driving the nation apart, a wedge that only grew deeper with time.

Directions:

1. Describe the below events using readings from your textbook.
2. Describe the purpose and effect of the Missouri Compromise, the Kansas-Nebraska Act, and the Lincoln Douglas Debates.
3. For each, answer: did this offer a durable, long-term solution to the controversy of slavery?

The Missouri Compromise

The Kansas Nebraska Act and "Bleeding Kansas"

The Lincoln Douglas Debates

Do Now

Use your knowledge of the Missouri Compromise, the Kansas Nebraska Act (and the Bleeding Kansas episode), and the Lincoln Douglas Debates to interpret and explain Thomas Jefferson's quote:

But as it is, we have the *wolf by the ear*, and we can neither hold him, nor safely let him go. Justice is in one scale, and self-preservation in the other. . . . We have the *wolf by the ears* and feel the danger of either holding or letting him loose.

Part 2: A Political Breakdown

Abraham Lincoln's election in 1860 lead to the rapid secession of seven states from the union, with four more to follow in the ensuing months.

Do Now

Using your knowledge of the Lincoln Douglas Debates and a close reading of Abraham Lincoln's Peoria Speech, offer an explanation of why southern states seceded from the union after his victory in 1860.

Part 3: Considering a Different Path

Offer an alternative history of the United States that does not include Civil War. What would have needed to change to avoid war? Describe the changes in detail and justify each by noting their effects.

Final Discussion: Was the American Civil War Inevitable?
Directions: Using your knowledge gained from this class, offer a 2–3 paragraph response to the question: was the American Civil War inevitable?

Example Assignment #4: Should the US Government Pay Reparations to African Americans and Native Americans?

Part 1: Research the Origins of African Slavery in North America

Directions: Answer the below question using research and close reading.

• How and why did Africans originally come to North American colonies and then the United States of America?
• Offer at least one paragraph explaining WHY, AND one paragraph explaining HOW. Share whole class, identifying the places where your accounts conflict and the places where your accounts overlap.
• Write a Class Response to the question, which will include statements agreed to by every member of the class.

Think and Write: Was the way in which African Americans were brought to the United States justified? How, if at all, can we right that wrong today?

Part 2: Should the Federal Government Pay African Americans Reparations for Slavery?

Directions: Read the articles assigned to you, take notes, and be prepared to present your answers to the following questions to the class:

1. What is the author's thesis? Put it in your own words.
2. Share 2–3 of the author's supporting arguments for this thesis—how does the author support his thesis with evidence and logic?
3. Do you agree with the author's thesis? Why or why not?

    a. If not, be prepared to offer specific repudiations of the author's logic
    b. If so, be ready to channel the precise arguments made by the author

RESOURCES

- An argument FOR reparations:
  "The Case for Reparations," by Ta-Nehisi Coates
  https://www.theatlantic.com/magazine/archive/2014/06/the-case-for-reparations/361631/?gclid=Cj0KCQiA7qP9BRCLARIsABDa
  ZzgrxOJsYB3wNUErMWIXsQRMg_aVqc8OVSChsxzqJy2YIeg
  zfrXpzpwaAsqXEALw_wcB
- An argument AGAINST reparations:
  "The Impossibility of Reparations," by David Frum
  https://www.theatlantic.com/business/archive/2014/06/the-impossibility-of-reparations/372041/

PRESENT YOUR AUTHOR'S CASE TO THE CLASS

1. Prepare to share your author's argument to the class and be ready to answer questions from your peers and me.
2. As your classmates share their author's arguments, take close notes on the arguments that come from the article you did NOT read.

a. You may be required to channel the arguments you're hearing in our next activity.

Part 3: Make a Case

Directions: Each of you will be randomly assigned the "yes" or "no" side of our debate question. Once assigned, you will prepare a 2–3 minute long statement offering arguments for your position. There will be a period reserved for cross-questioning, in which members of the other group will have the opportunity to ask you clarifying questions and challenge your contentions.

Below is a list of questions for teachers that can serve as the basis for lesson plans, with brief descriptions of the issues at stake below the questions. Please use them as you like.

1. Was the American belief in Manifest Destiny defensible from a global perspective? Was it ultimately good for both the nation and the world?

   a. No: In our zeal to control the North American continent, the United States government and American citizens murdered and displaced millions of Native Americans and started a war with Mexico as a pretext for annexing its northern territories. The American obsession with Manifest Destiny led to staggering human costs for non-Americans.

   b. Yes: Innovation in the United States in the twentieth and twenty-first centuries has lifted the material quality of life for millions around the planet. Our medical innovations alone have saved countless lives. Moreover, US willingness to be the standard-bearer for liberal democracy has contributed to global democratization for decades (a trend that, admittedly, has been in decline for the past ten years). Finally, the demand for goods created by the American economy and the protection that the US government offers the world (in the form of guaranteeing safe trade routes, paying for the defense of Europe, Japan, and others, etc.) has been a catalyst for global growth since World War II. Without such a large, well-secured territory, it's unlikely that the United States would have been able to offer these benefits to the world.

2. Was the New Deal's expansion of the role and powers of the federal government ultimately beneficial for the nation?

   a. Yes: The New Deal provided essential services to Americans when it was most needed, and set the precedent for large-scale intervention from the federal government in the lives of Americans. Social Security, which has all but eliminated elderly poverty, is just one example of a program that has unequivocally improved quality of life for Americans.

   b. No: FDR's New Deal created an unwieldy and unaccountable administrative state that—outside of a few distinctive programs like Social Security—fails to efficiently provide services that truly improve quality of life for most Americans. Further, the expansion of the federal government that FDR's New Deal kicked off has driven taxes up and put our nation on a path toward insolvency.

3. Was the Patriot Act justified?

   a. Yes: The 9/11 terrorist attacks took us by surprise, and the government must do what's necessary to prevent anything like it from happening again. Protecting the safety of its citizens is the first priority of any government, and the Patriot Act allows the government to better do so. While the act does infringe on the individual liberties of certain Americans, securing our nation's safety comes first. Without a stable country, nobody has individual liberty—that's why safety comes first.

   b. No: The United States of America's most cherished values are individual liberty and limited government, and the Patriot Act violates both in the name of protecting national security, a vague and sweeping mandate that—given the longstanding, serious threats to the nation—can nearly always be invoked. The federal government can keep Americans safe without violating our fundamental right to privacy. Individual liberty—the bedrock of the American philosophy and identity—cannot be so flippantly sacrificed in the name of vague "safety."

TEACHING DEBATE THROUGH
US GOVERNMENT AND ECONOMICS

The bedrock values that defines the United States exist in a state of perpetual tension. Here are just a few examples:

1. How are we to simultaneously follow the will of the majority (the defining principle of democracy) and protect the rights of minorities (the basic goal of individual sovereignty)?
2. When faced with challenging decisions, should our representatives follow the will of their constituents, their own values, or their party's preferences?
3. How can we possibly guarantee individual freedom and pursue social equality at the same time?

Active citizens need to understand the values that underpin our government and economy well enough to recognize the inherent tensions that exists within them, and then decide how to balance their sometimes competing and sometimes complementary mandates. We as a nation can't agree on when it's acceptable for the government to intervene in our private lives, when we should promote democracy abroad, and how to respond to those who disrespect our flag. The very definitions of citizenship and freedom are not settled in this country, despite the pervasiveness of the words in political discourse.

Framing the subjects of US government and economics as a series of important debates about how we should live together captures their spirit, since their core content—the US Constitution and Declaration of Independence, the Federalist Papers, the Wealth of Nations, The Theory of Moral Sentiments, and other treatises and theories—leave plenty of room for interpretation and grapple with these contradictions themselves. Our core documents and founding debates demonstrate how our nation has clashed over questions over how to balance security and freedom, how to increase equality without infringing on individual liberty, and how to balance power between Congress and the presidency, from the beginning.

To avoid the debates and ambiguities inherent in economics and governments is to mislead our students about these subjects. It's also boring: the difference between a lecture and a series of questions about what type of society we want to live in. Of course, instructors have to unequivocally explain how the economy and government operate to young people, but they should also ask them to share their opinions on these structures and emphasize the unsettled nature of many of our most important governing questions. Framing civics content as debates is both engaging and accurate, capturing students' attentions and the spirit of the subjects. This method also invites students to contribute to our shared understanding of what it means to be American, and helps them see the necessity of their thoughtful contributions going forward.

Civil debate—the competition of ideas within a self-governing community—is at the very core of democratic citizenship. It's the engine that propels democracies forward and enables them to progress. And the sacred responsibility to teach the habits and skills necessary for rigorous, open-minded debate falls to schools, the civic institutions charged with developing the next generation of American citizens.

DEBATABLE LESSON TOPICS FOR US GOVERNMENT AND ECONOMICS

"Essential questions" have become increasingly popular among educators in the humanities and social sciences. These are questions that anchor content, guide inquiry, and organize student thinking—they are questions that students will be able to answer by the end of the class, unit, semester, or year using newly learned content. "Essential questions" are engaging and debatable, and while they cannot be cleanly answered in full, they can be more fully understood and commented on by those with knowledge of course content.

"Essential questions" are powerful tools for organizing and presenting civic content (starting from elementary school civic and local history courses, through high school AP government and economics classes and into social science courses at universities) because they capture the fundamentally debatable and ambiguous nature of American citizenship. Perhaps the overarching "essential question" of US civics courses, the one that organizes the subjects within it and from which all other essential questions flow is, "What should American citizens do?" By framing the study of civics as a question rather than a statement, we communicate the subject's debatable nature and invite students to participate as both consumers and contributors.

The truth is that we as a nation are perpetually refining our understanding of citizenship—what should we expect from one another, the government, and the economy—through dialogue and debate, and one responsibility of the American citizen is to contribute to that debate. But contributing to a national dialogue on the question of how we should all live together takes skill and prior knowledge, and using essential questions that force students to contribute to the national project rather than simply receive information about it prepares them for the active life of an American citizen.

Below are a series of essential questions for the subjects of government and economics that will guide students' thinking as they learn new content. Teachers can use these questions and lesson planning ideas to boost student engagement in what might otherwise be perceived to be dry material. At its root, civics deals with morality. It's the subject of how we can live together most happily, and in pursuing civic virtue we are pursuing nothing short of collective excellence.

The following essential questions, then, ask students to make value judgments, to decide how a policy that benefits one group and harms another should be judged, how much to expect from fellow citizens, how our institutions should use their powers, and many more questions that together help us answer the essential question that defines American civics: "What should US citizens do?"

Government

When Should the Majority Rule?

The difference between "democracy" and "populism" usually depends on whether you're on the side of the group making all the noise. Populism refers to mass political movements that run against the values of a free society. Populist movements tend to be xenophobic, rooted in resentment at a changing country, and in need of a charismatic leader and obvious enemy. They believe that the force of their movement is more important than the individual rights at the heart of democratic governments, so they might advocate for restricting the rights of immigrants, adjusting the term limits of their leaders, or silencing critics.

But populist movements are also . . . popular. That is, driven by a large group of people with considerable collective power. The very democratic processes that put the people in the driver's seat also open the door to some questionable driving. Many representatives ride populist movements to power and are willing to take orders from the masses in order to stay there. But our democracy depends on enough politicians not doing that, and sometimes siding with democratic norms over the demands of their constituents.

The founders knew that the US public couldn't be relied upon to consistently uphold the liberal democratic values they enshrined in the US Constitution and Declaration of Independence—that's why they took such pains to insulate the federal judiciary from "the capriciousness of the masses." But sometimes even the politicians, whose careers depend on the popularity contests that are elections, must ignore their constituents. When should they do that? And when, more generally, should the will of the majority not prevail?

This line of inquiry helps students think through the indispensable roles of both the public and governing experts in a democracy, and forces them to reflect on a fundamental assumption of democratic government: that the people are wise.

What Are the Causes and Effects of Political Polarization?

Many of the challenges facing our society today tell us a great deal about human nature. Political polarization is a type of atomized nationalism, where Americans develop a sense of intense loyalty to a subsection of the country that's claiming to represent the "real" America. After spending enough time with fellow partisans and consuming a media diet that vilifies and patronizes the Other, too many of us have come to view our fellow Americans primarily as antagonists who mean us harm. This phenomenon is driven by the natural human tendency to find tribes that lend us a sense of identity and make us feel like we are a part of the in-group.

We are tribal creatures at root, naturally intolerant of differences and wary of alternative lifestyles—that's why civic education's mandate of teaching tolerance and compromise is so essential and so hard. Liberal values are unnatural in the human brain, we have to override more primal impulses to make them stick. But when enough of us succeed in instilling tolerance and open-mindedness into our worldviews and habits, we all live better lives.

Today, our hard-wired tendencies toward group-think and polarization are enflamed by a decentralized media environment that makes it easier to lodge ourselves in "echo-chambers" that incentivize doubling-down on rather than questioning our political beliefs. The darker, less tolerant side of our nature has been handed a microphone and eager crowd by the internet and social media, phenomena that incentivize us to harshen our rhetoric de-incentivizes attempts at understanding and moderation.

The Greeks, channeled by Robert Kennedy in 1968, summarized the goal of society, which is about "taming the savageness of man, and making gentle the life of this world." It's the deeply natural—and in their untouched state—savage parts of us that seek the comfort of atomized political identities, forged in warlike opposition to Americans with different policy preferences. And it's an education steeped in the American values of compromise, liberty, tolerance, and inquiry that curb the primitive impulses to attack those who are different from us and bring out the "better angels of our nature."

Students should be encouraged to find solutions to political polarization—how can they, in their daily decisions, reduce political polarization in their own lives? And what of the causes of this polarization? Students will likely be able to comment on how political affiliations influence their personal lives—few of us have been able to escape heated political exchanges at the dinner table over the past few years. But students can also be offered examples of how partisan politics affects the policy-making process (by leading to more partisan legislation when one party is in power and gridlock when power is shared), and then reflect on how these effects alter their lives.

Rather than simply communicating the trend toward party polarization over the past several decades, US government teachers should ask students to develop their own causal theories that explain party polarization, assess its affects, and propose solutions. Polarization is a defining feature of our society and government today, and students should be considering its origins and effects on their lives frequently.

Finally, by pointing out the phenomenon of partisanship to young people, we offer them an opportunity to analyze rather than simply submit to its pull. This essential question helps young people take a step back and decide whether they want to vilify those who hold opposing political views, or whether they'd rather seek to identify as Americans rather than Democrats or Republicans. By presenting students the opportunity to rigorously reflect on this fundamental feature of American politics today, and calling on them to assess the effects of partisanship on them personally, their neighbors, and on the nation as a whole, we call them back to that overarching essential question in civic education: "What should American citizens do?"

When Should Individual Liberty Be Sacrificed for Social Order and National Security?

There is no balancing act more important to free societies than the one that allows them to guarantee order and liberty simultaneously. Those of us who have lived in nations that lack basic order, nations in which crime is rampant and your person and possessions are under constant threat by others, can attest to the truism that "order is like air—when it's there you never think of it, and when it's not you can't think of anything else." Anarchy is a horror that governments—the entities with monopolies on the use of violence—successfully end. And when they fail to do so, we describe them straightforwardly as "failed states."

Perhaps governments, which use coercion to organize people, are humanity's most important innovation, as the conditions they create enable nearly all other innovations. In the chaos that is anarchy, the state described by the great Thomas Hobbes as a "war, each against all," the innovations that have improved humanity's quality of life would have been impossible (imagine Steve Jobs creating the aesthetics of the iPhone in a war zone).

For centuries, people lived under governments that saw their primary directive as maintaining social stability at all costs, and democratic citizens would (and ought to) turn their noses up at those governing models. By the standards of liberal democracy, order is necessary but not sufficient. Governments focused on establishing order rescue us from anarchy but engender the threat of tyranny, which has just as crushing an effect on the human spirit. The question the American founders grappled with more than any other is how to structure a government that guarantees both social stability (we need not fear one another) and individual freedom (we need not fear the state).

Predictably, James Madison put the problem more eloquently: "In framing a government, which is to be administered by men over men, the great difficulty is this: You must first enable the government to control the governed; and in the next place, oblige it to control itself." The founders feared tyranny over nearly all else, and they devised a governing system that is remarkably effective at combating it by disaggregating power through a tiered federalist structure, erecting a system of checks and balances, and offering myriad opportunities for the public to hold leaders accountable. They did this in service of individual liberty and were profoundly successful.

But even our founding fathers who so feared the shadow of tyranny recognized that individual liberties were not absolute. They knew that sometimes the government would need to infringe on our personal rights for the sake of national security and social stability, which is why presidents have the power to act unilaterally during emergencies, Congress can tax its people, and any of us can be put in jail for violating the social contract. Every thoughtful American citizen must understand that the twin goals of liberty and security will exist in a state of perpetual tension, each gnawing and grating on the other, each uncomfortable with the mandate of the other. Most importantly, young people must see that there is no neat formula that allows us to cleanly balance individual liberty and security in our society, that the question of which principle should win depends on the scenario, that the relationship has been continuously revisited and revised throughout US history.

Case studies on this balance abound, but the most engaging one I've ever used revolve around the Patriot Act (does it violate the fourth amendment? If it does, is such a violation justified by 9/11?) and *The New York Times vs. US Government* Supreme Court case in 1971. Teachers could just as easily enthrall students with the cases of Edward Snowden and Julian Assange, as the two cases together offer ample evidence for either order or liberty carrying the day.

But for students the most important point is that these two principles, ever at each other's throats, require ongoing mediation. The best form of American democracy balances order and liberty, and the next generation must decide what that means.

Economics

When Should the Federal Reserve Raise Interest Rates?

It's easy to simply tell students that monetary policy is set by the Federal Reserve, which is mandated by Congress to pursue the twins goals of achieving full employment and price stability (where inflation is at roughly 2 percent per year), then describe their instruments for achieving those goals, and then move on. But skilled civics teachers will draw students' attention to the tradeoffs associated with pursuing one goal over the other, as oftentimes full employment can create price instability by driving inflation up. So, should the Federal Reserve err on the side of keeping interest rates low to drive employment, or raise them to forestall the threat of inflation? Do we want more people employed and higher prices, or vice versa? Who benefits when the Federal Reserve achieves one goal but not the other? How do prices affect us all? How does the unemployment rate affect us all?

Is the Minimum Wage an Effective Tool for Boosting Collective Prosperity?

Rather than pointing out the inefficiencies that arise from price ceilings (like rent control) and price floors (like the minimum wage) and then moving on, economics teachers might ask students to consider tangible effects of that most famous of price floors: the minimum wage. Does the cost that the minimum wage imposes on businesses justify the heightened quality of life that it offers workers? If businesses do go bust because of a raised minimum wage, who is affected outside of the owners and employees? Are customers substantially affected? Are other businesses dependent on that failed business?

Could businesses harmed or destroyed by a burdensome minimum wage affect you? How? Should the low wage earners who benefit from a raise in the minimum wage be prioritized over business owners? Why or why not? Does the increased spending power of those who see their wages rise from an increased minimum wage drive broader economic growth? Where do they spend their extra money? Might their heightened spending benefit other businesses?

After considering the moral and theoretical arguments for and against an ever-rising minimum wage, young people should look at data that communicates actual effects of the minimum wage on the economy. Teachers might guide their students through economic data with these questions:

When the minimum wage was first introduced, how did that affect the economy and the owners that make it up? What happened when it was raised? After analyzing the tradeoffs, would students support a raised minimum wage? Why or why not?

Should Governments Allow Corporations to Hire Foreign Workers Abroad for Substantially Less Pay?

Like most important questions in economics, this one requires students to investigate the elaborate web of interconnectivity that defines our world today. The ability of corporations to hire talent from abroad for a far lower price tag affects far more people that just US and foreign job-seekers. Perhaps this practice is what has allowed corporations that add tremendous value to US consumers to have gotten off the ground in the first place? Maybe it's enabled them to lower prices for American consumers on a vast array of goods. But maybe if Americans had landed more of jobs that have been offshored, their domestic spending would have spawned the creation of whole new American businesses that would now be empowering consumers and offering new sorts of jobs we can't even imagine.

Asking students to develop, share, and defend policy positions that are both complex and materially important forces them to really under-stand the subtleties and intricate trade-offs that are an unshakeable feature of the American government and economy. The American economy is a hard thing to understand, yet US political parties simplify economic policy into a series of slogans that energize without explain-ing, that move people to march rather than inquire. Ultimately, eco-nomics teachers must communicate that the subject is more layered than partisan politics allows, and instill a since of awe at the profound interconnection between stakeholders in the US and global economies.

To recap, there are three reasons for schools presenting US history, government, economics, and the subject of civics at large as an ongoing debate:

1. It's accurate. The meaning of our history and national values have always been debated. Debate over our common values and the lessons to be learned from our national history is baked into our collective identity. In a very important sense, our national identity is tied to debate. It also forces inevitably biased individ-uals (that's us) from passing our biases down to the next genera-tion.

2. It's engaging. Inviting students to debate the meaning of our history and governing values involves them in that history and government. Rather than casting them as passive receptacles of knowledge, this teaching method forces students to contribute to

our 260-year-long national discussion on the role of our government and the meaning of our history. It forces them to be active members of our democracy, not mere spectators.

3. It offers a positive, widely relatable national identity—an uplifting answer to the question of what unites us as Americans. The answer: we're in the process of figuring that out, as we've always been, *and it's this process that defines us*. What makes our nation a "we" is our commitment to together continue to build a more perfect union

Chapter Two

Rule #2

Teach Renewal as a Core American Value

America is a moving target, a goal that must always be pursued and never quite reached. As it has moved, it has expanded rights—for blacks, for other minority groups, for women, for the LGBTQ community, for others who have been oppressed—and revisited the question of what it means to provide equality before the law. This is not just the right thing to do but the smart thing. America works best when it gives people the freedom to tap their own energies and exploit their talents. — Thomas E. Ricks

Consider a stagnant pond and a rushing river. The pond languishes in relative peace—there isn't much discord, because there isn't much movement. It's a predictable, enervated body that possesses the tranquility of death.

Ponds do change, with droughts they shrink and with rains they grow. But these changes are dependent on large, powerful, indifferent external forces. Lacking the capacity for self-renewal, the pond's only options are to wait for alien, detached powers to infuse it with life, or slowly die.

Rivers, by contrast, can be choppy, temperamental, and unpredictable. They move in ways that are sometimes serene and sometimes disruptive. They can be defined by their endemic vitality, which is sustained by the unceasing movement of new water, minerals, and wildlife.

Authoritarian governments create societies like ponds, societies that lack an endemic means for renewal. Change tends to comes from the top down, from powerful, centralized, seemingly (from the perch of someone outside the halls of power) random forces that wield tremendous power. Citizens are cut off from government power, and so lose the ability to change their own living conditions and those of their children. Rather than being able to chart their own course, lead the lives they like, and influence the national direction, people under authoritarian regimes must wait for those above them to make decisions and hope for the best.

Over half of the nations across the globe are stuck in this state of stunted development, a state in which the vast majority of their residents lack control over their lives and the nation's. The standard authoritarian arrangement concentrates power in the tip of the social pyramid, walling the decision-maker off from outside influence. In doing so, these regimes rob themselves and their nation of its most powerful force for creativity, innovation, and vitality: the people.

DEMOCRATIC DYNAMISM

The great strength of democratic governments is their endemic ability to evolve, a power fueled by their connection to the people. If authoritarian regimes create pond-like societies, democracies resemble rivers.

Democratic nations are bodies in states of constant and controlled flux, ever-renewed by the perpetual inflow of new ideas and people. While bound by their physical contours, rivers burst with novelty and vitality and can support diverse and new forms of life. Rivers, then, are stable bodies undergoing a process of perpetual internal renewal. They embrace and are defined by the inevitability of change, and can support vibrant arrays of life as a result. Democratic constitutions and founding principles act as river banks, joining the creative energy of the people with the democratic liberal ideas at the heart of their national identity.

Ponds lack new inflows, relying on the same water to support life for years at a time—with markedly less success than rivers. Aging dictators and their governing cabals make for stale rulers—their administrations are stagnant by definition. They reward loyalty rather than talent, and consider change a threat to their power. They lack the river's capacity for self-renewal, and therefore lack its dynamism and vitality.

For centuries, human society was more pond than river. Large changes to the social order came from the edicts of kings and emperors—a powerful elite who viewed themselves as separate from the masses. The culture of the general public did evolve and grow, but those cultural changes were cut off from the state, which was beholden to the culture and values of the elites that controlled it. With policymakers cut off from the creative energy of their citizens, governments lacked dynamism and were incapable of responding to changes in their nation with anything other than brute force. Human society became more complex and rich, but at an achingly slow pace that did not reflect the creative energies of the human spirit and did not come close to rivaling the rate of social change in today's democracies.

Where autocratic governments work to separate themselves from the chaotic and creative energy of the masses, democracy is designed to harness that energy. By joining the powers of the state with the ever-churning will of the people, democracies infuse their governments and societies with vitality, and position themselves to grow and adapt in ways that are unthinkable under any other form of government. This adaptability is a tremendous advantage and is responsible for the historically unprecedented prosperity and stability of democratic nations across the world.

If there is one core value embedded in democratic governments, it's renewal. A system grounded in the will of the people may at times be unstable and chaotic, but it will never be stagnant and unresponsive. Democratic governments' great source of strength is their capacity to change with the will of the people, and to harness the creative energy of humanity. Lacking this endemic nimbleness, top-down governments fear social change and must use cruelty and manipulation to dampen it.

And while such societies may persist, they cannot flourish. Humanity's great strength is its ability to adapt to new circumstances, to learn—and to use what we learn to improve our lives. Democracies allow society to change itself by attaching the will of the people to the arms of the state. Without democracy, the vibrancy and creative potential of human beings is cut off from the policy-making process. Again, the foundational value of democracy—more than freedom, equality, or individualism—is renewal. It's time we celebrated that principle in our schools.

THE UNITED STATES: THE NATION OF DEMOCRATIC RENEWAL

While democracies abound around the world (though they are a slim minority to non-democracies) there is no question that the United States—as the oldest and most famous republic—has a special relationship with democratic ethos. Our nation was birthed from a desire for individual sovereignty, and our founding documents articulate a theory of government that renders all forms of government that are not "dependent on the people" illegitimate.

The American Revolution would have been a mere power grab by colonial aristocrats if not for the powerful insights into human nature and novel governing structures it proposed. Our national identity depends on the political philosophy articulated in the opening lines of the Declaration of Independence and the elegant distribution of power laid out in the US Constitution. Some nations have the advantage of ethnic and cultural similarities. Some have thousands of years of history. The United States is bound together by a passionate commitment to a democratic theory that insists that governments exist to serve the people (not the other way around), and as such must be dependent on the people. The American bedrock principles of popular sovereignty, individual liberty, rule of law, and equality create the conditions necessary for that other, rarely mentioned American principle: popular renewal.

The central democratic value is renewal—the power of democracy is its ability to catch the winds of human innovation for the benefit of us all. When you link the government with the people, you make government responsive to their innovations. Where most regimes must repress society's impulses for change, democracies can take advantage of them. Our nation's ability to grow and renew itself is at the heart of our identity. It's time that we as a nation begin to emphasize that alongside our much celebrated values of freedom and equality. Schools, the most important culture-making institutions in the nation, the one with the widest reach in American life, are the natural place to begin exposing our young citizens to this overlooked value.

Perhaps the most forceful, elegant, and impactful statement about the relationship between individuals and the state come in the opening lines of the Declaration of Independence:

> We hold these truths to be self-evident, that all men are created equal, that they are endowed by their Creator with certain unalienable Rights,

that among these are Life, Liberty and the pursuit of Happiness.–That to secure these rights, Governments are instituted among Men, deriving their just powers from the consent of the governed, –That whenever any Form of Government becomes destructive of these ends, it is the Right of the People to alter or to abolish it, and to institute new Government, laying its foundation on such principles and organizing its powers in such form, as to them shall seem most likely to effect their Safety and Happiness.

These lines unmistakably thrust the powers of the government into the hands of the people. And "the people," so vast and vibrant, will continuously alter the nation, renewing it with each generation.

TEACHING AMERICAN LIBERAL DEMOCRACY'S ANTI-DEMOCRATIC FEATURES

While American liberal democracy—with its plethora of public offices, frequent elections, and common use of referendums—offers incalculable opportunity for public influence, it also contains structures that deflect and outright block public opinion from fully taking the reins of state. The founders were deeply concerned with the potentially destructive effect of "the tyranny of the majority" on a stable, tolerant society. They worried that a mass of humanity—largely uneducated and susceptible to what psychologists today might call "group think"—tasked with steering a nation may use their powers in illiberal, unwise, or outright tyrannical ways.

To soften our worst impulses, American Liberal Democracy insists on the rule of law upheld by a judicial branch that is insulated from the pressures of public opinion, a president limited to two terms (even if he is popular enough to win more), and an upper legislative chamber explicitly designed to be relatively removed from the seesawing intensity of the people's will, to name a few. Such anti-democratic features may appear to fly in the face of my claim that our capacity for people-driven social renewal is at the core of the American governing philosophy and national identity. What role do the 870 federal judges, nominated by the president, confirmed by the senate, and serving lifetime terms, play in this government that is so ostensibly dependent on the will of the people?

I've found sharing this type of a question with my students to be very fruitful, as it hoists an apparent contradiction upon them and then forces them to resolve it. Younger students may respond better to a prompt along the lines of, "When should the government NOT listen to the people?" The notion that democratic citizens can't solve every problem may sound new and radical to some students, and can lead to some meaningful discussions about the role of authority and expertise in governing. Does the general public always know best? When should experts, rather than the people, make decisions? What would happen if students rather than teachers set classroom rules? These are compelling questions that will prompt important debate and discussion.

Democracies are governed by majorities, and democratic politics is the perpetual battle to persuade a majority of constituents to follow a particular set of policies and positions. And while government by majority is more inclusive than government of one, it is not always more enlightened. Majorities have prejudices. They may resent minorities and take actions to curb their rights. In a democratic nation without the rule of law, rulers backed by a majority of the people in their nation may come to resemble autocrats—they could terrorize disempowered ethnic groups, intimidate opponents using the powers of the state, and even take steps to undermine future elections to ensure that they retain power. And they could do all this in the name of the people, with the support of the majority.

Recognizing the threat of the "tyranny of the majority" lead the founders to include the "Bill of Rights" in the US Constitution, which protect the individual liberties of all Americans, no matter how unpopular or hated those people may be, and thereby curbs the power of democratic majorities. And it's those 870 unelected federal judges that we trust to protect our freedoms, and we can trust them to do so precisely because their roles do not depend on majority approval. If they were, they'd be tempted to slam the law onto their enemies and lift it for their friends. Rule of law and constitutional government places some limits on popular rule, but it's also those limits that breathe life into popular rule in the first place.

By constraining the intensity of popular movements with constitutional principles protected by unelected experts, the rule of law allows democracy to flourish. Only a stable nation can really harness democratic creativity and innovation. A weak nation would be rocked by it. It's the river with well-buttressed, high banks that is best able to channel the torrents of change; one that is not firmly enough bound (as our nation is by its constitution) would be overrun by new inflows and lose its capacity for ongoing renewal.

But while a judicial branch of professionals and legal experts can help stabilize democracies, true popular government requires a public that is fit to rule—a public that can passionately advance their own interests while respecting the interests of others. It's a public that can hold strong beliefs, but still compromise with their political opponents because they understand that democratic government does not function without compromise. And their highest loyalty is not to their own personal political values, but to the democratic values that enable political expression and popular rule—that allow them to have political disagreements that mean anything in the first place.

HOW TRADITIONAL AMERICAN VALUES COMBINE WITH THE VALUE OF RENEWAL

The energizing notion that new generations of Americans can and must stamp their values onto the country assumes that Americans across generations will share a basic set of assumptions about how to treat one another and collectively steer the nation. The bounds within which generational renewal can take place are enumerated by the Declaration of Independence and US Constitution and clarified and expanded upon by seminal American documents (*The Federalist Papers*, *Letter from a Birmingham Jail*, etc.), landmark Supreme Court decisions (*Brown vs. Board of Education*, *New York Times vs. United States*, etc.), and historic legislation (The Civil Rights Act of 1964, The Voting Rights Act of 1965, etc.).

Young people should reconsider and reassess the meaning and application of American values articulated by previous generations, but renewing them should almost never mean overhauling them. American liberal values are the framework within meaningful change can take place, and guide every generation's pursuit of progress and justice. Our nation values are ambiguous and lofty by design—they're meant to be continuously reinterpreted and reconsidered. Young people should be pushed to consider and reconsider our basic values, looking at how they've been applied (or ignored) in the past, and determining what they mean today. Here are just a few of the questions that young people should consider before taking the reins of society:

1. Do social welfare programs contribute or detract from a free society?

2. Does the principle of "equality" demand special treatment for historically oppressed groups, or instead require equivalent treatment for all regardless of background?
3. When do national security concerns justify violating American's right to personal privacy as guaranteed by the fourth amendment?
4. Does the equal protections clause of the fourteenth amendment—passed in the wake of the Civil War to guarantee full citizenship to black Americans—apply to an unborn fetus?
5. Should the United States attempt to spread liberal democratic values abroad?

To insist that future generations commit to fundamental American values is far less constricting than it sounds at first brush, as the meaning of these values have been debated and expanded throughout American history. There are some basic behaviors that they unequivocally reject, but mostly they're silent on specifics. They leave that to us, those who are inspired by them and then responsible for giving them life.

AN EXAMPLE OF TYRANNY OF THE MAJORITY AND ITS REMEDY: GERRYMANDERING

While international examples of coercive majorities abound, we are also not free of majoritarian abuses at home. Gerrymandering is the process of state legislatures redrawing electoral districts to favor the dominant party in an upcoming election. It's the majority using its power now to guarantee power later, designing districts to suit the desires of the representatives rather than the desires of the constituents. Despite the blatantly anti-democratic nature of the practice—it has been widely panned as representatives choosing their voters rather than voters choosing their representatives—it persists in the majority of states today.

Such practices force faithful believers in democracy to face an uncomfortable question: how can we prevent democratically elected officials from turning a one-time political minority (the one that lost the initial election) into a perennial minority? How do we curb the powers of legislative majorities?

When majority rule can't be trusted, Americans turn to the courts, which are designed to be blind to the prejudices of public opinion. In the 1962 landmark Supreme Court case *Baker vs. Carr*, justices ruled that, as neutral bodies whose powers are not dependent on elections, federal courts are the entities most suited to adjudicate electoral disputes and draw electoral districts. Such is the logic of our judicial system, which is administered by unelected legal professionals and focuses on understanding facts rather than championing ideas and promoting policy preferences.

Most Americans intuitively understand that the law must be universally applied and deaf to the preferences of those in power, and that elections are all about capturing the hearts of the majority for the sake of gaining political power.

Since laws are blind to particulars, and judges are tasked with applying rather than making the law, it's judges who are most often tasked with protecting the rights of minorities who might otherwise face discrimination from a hostile majority. If elections were our only metric for measuring what's right and wrong, minorities would face an unceasing threat of abuse, future elections would be predetermined by those past, and the nation would be ruled by the (sometimes tyrannical) whims of the 51 percent. Luckily, our nation lives by deeper principles that the changing tides of majority opinion, principles that—at their best—guide majority opinion, but at the very least constrain it. Those principles are enumerated in the Bill of Rights and reinforced by judges and lawyers, who act as guardians to the rule of law, which is blessedly indifferent to popular opinion.

By emphasizing the underappreciated yet fundamental value of *renewal* to young people, civics educators invite them to contribute to the American experiment. Our national health depends on their contribution in two simple ways: first, by reinterpreting our national values and priorities and holding us accountable to our founding principles; and second, by vigorously and wisely contributing to public life.

LESSON PLANS: US HISTORY AND GOVERNMENT

Below are lesson plans that highlight the American value of renewal. Like the lesson plans in chapter 1, these are intended to be modified for timing and grade level.

Assignment #1: US History

Tracing the Right to Vote Through American History

Essential Questions:

- HOW has the right to vote been expanded throughout American history (who championed it, and through what means)?
- WHY has the right to vote been expanded throughout American history (how is expanded enfranchisement consistent with American values)?

Part 1: How Has the Right to Vote Changed from 1789 to 2020?

Research and Draw: Draw a timeline that charts how the right to vote expanded to new groups between 1789 and 2020. After completing the timeline, answer: Which groups still lack the right to vote in 2020?

Part 2: What Effect Has the Expansion of the Ballot Had on American Society?

Directions: Answer the above question using:

  a. Two politicians (those who won with a large percentage of voters who were previously ineligible)
  b. Two laws (passed to serve populations that previously didn't have the right to vote)
  c. How would the United States be different today if the right to vote had NOT been dramatically expanded throughout our history? Offer a counter-factual historical narrative.

Part 3: American Values and Voting Rights

Point to Ponder: Based on what you just learned about how voting has changed throughout American history, what lesson should we draw about American principles, government, and democracy? What can the history of the ballot tell us about the United States?

Assignment #2: Analyzing Fundamental and Vague Language

> *We the People of the United States, in Order to form a more perfect Union, establish Justice, insure domestic Tranquility, provide for the common defence, promote the general Welfare, and secure the Blessings of Liberty to ourselves and our Posterity, do ordain and establish this Constitution for the United States of America.*

Directions

1. Read the preamble to the US Constitution above closely.
2. Based on your reading, answer the following:

> a. What does the preamble tell you about the values of our nation?
>
> > a. Hint: WHO is establishing this nation, governed by this Constitution?
> > b. What is the PURPOSE of the Constitution? What are its goals?

3. How do the values of the preamble relate to the history of voting rights in the United States?

Consider the Facts, Then Share Your Perspective

The Preamble to the United States Constitution clearly points to the origin of the document— "We the people." The very first words affirm that it was the people, not a removed elite who inspired (though, admittedly did not write) the Constitution, and it's the people whom it will serve. The next phrase establishes the goal of the document, which is first to "establish a more perfect union." The phrase "more perfect" has long been interpreted to mean that the Constitution as it was written, and the United States as it existed at the time of its writing—1789— was incomplete. Rather than establish an untouchable end-state, the US Constitution is a framework that enables the American people to create an ever "more perfect" nation.

Our Constitution creates a process through which Americans can shape their nation—it is the means by which "we the people" can collectively build an ever "more perfect" social and political union. The expansion of voting rights from propertied white males only to nearly every citizen with at least eighteen years under their belts is a powerful example of this philosophy being realized. It was Americans who amended our Constitution to expand a once-exclusive right to the ballot, one group at a time. And with each expansion, the next became easier—with more people participating in the political process, bringing more and more people into that process became philosophically inevitable and practically easier.

VOTING RIGHTS AND AMERICAN DEMOCRATIC PRINCIPLES: TURN AND TALK

What values and principles does the history of voting rights in American point to? Deduce 2–3 principles and values from this history. What does the expansion of voting rights say about what the United States values and believes in?

Think and Write: In your own words, describe how the principle of social renewal has altered US history.

Extension Assignment(s): Finding Democratic Renewal in American History

Directions: Identify more examples where the American Democratic Principle of Renewal reveals itself in American history.

Example Areas of Study:

1. From the Articles of Confederation to the US Constitution
2. Westward Expansion
3. The Civil Rights Era

Extension Assignment #1: US Government

Essential Question: How have American social movements changed our understanding of core American values?

Directions for Split Research:

1. A third of the class will be assigned the Progressive Era, a third assigned the New Deal, and a third the Civil Rights Movement.
2. Identify two valuable primary sources and two secondary sources relevant to your movement.
3. Actively read them, with the below questions in mind:

    a. What were the movement's goals?
    b. Who were its leaders, and to whom did it appeal?
    c. What were the movement's accomplishments? How did it change life for Americans?
    d. To what extent did the movements challenge and change our definitions of equality and freedom? How do you define equality? Freedom?

4. Answer the above questions in writing, and prepare to share your answers to the class. You are responsible for communicating the events and impacts of your movement to the class.

    a. The rest of the class takes notes during presentations.

5. The class asks questions of the presenters and, once everyone is done, organizes notes to prepare for a discussion on the essential question.

Discussion:

1. Use what you know to answer the question you saw at the beginning of class: how have American social movements change our understanding of core American values? First answer in writing, drawing on all three social movements we recently learned of.
2. Share an idea briefly with the class, and a classmate will take public notes. Compile several different ways of answering the question.
3. Break into groups of 5–7 and discuss the essential question in detail. One person takes notes—are there any disagreements?
4. In your same groups, discuss the final questions: To what extent did the movements challenge and change our definitions of equality and freedom? How do you define equality? Freedom?

Extension Assignment #2: Tracing US Amendments: How Has Our Nation Grown?

Activity:
Directions:

1. Read all four of the below amendments, passed between 1919 and 1971.
2. Restate the meaning of each amendment in your own words: according to you, what did each do?
3. Identify a common pattern. How are all the amendments similar? What are they all aiming to do?

The Nineteenth Amendment

The right of citizens of the United States to vote shall not be denied or abridged by the United States or by any State on account of sex.

The Twenty-Second Amendment

No person shall be elected to the office of the President more than twice, and no person who has held the office of President, or acted as President, for more than two years of a term to which some other person was elected President shall be elected to the office of President more than once.

The Twenty-Fourth Amendment

The right of citizens of the United States to vote in any primary or other election for President or Vice President, for electors for President or Vice President, or for Senator or Representative in Congress, shall not be denied or abridged by the United States or any State by reason of failure to pay poll tax or other tax.

The Twenty-Sixth Amendment

The right of citizens of the United States, who are eighteen years of age or older, to vote shall not be denied or abridged by the United States or by any State on account of age.

Think, Pair, Share

Directions: First answer the below questions in writing, then share your responses with a partner, and finally share your partner's responses to the whole group.

1. How did the nineteenth, twenty-second, twenty-fourth, and twenty-sixth amendments together change American democracy? What was their general effect?
2. How did they change the relationship between voters and representatives?
3. Who benefitted from these four amendments, and what do those who benefitted have in common?

Extension Assignment #3: Tracing State Amendments: How Has Our State Grown Through the Amendment Process?

Investigating Our State's Amendments

Directions: Investigate your state's amendments, and answer:

1. How many amendments are there? How does my state's number of amendments compare to the number of US amendments? What might account for this difference?
2. What are the themes of the amendments? What are the amendments about, in general?
3. Choose 2–3 amendments that jump out at you and learn as much as you can about them. You'll present these amendments to the class.

    a. When were they passed?
    b. What events prompted their passing? What problems were they trying to solve?
    c. What is their effect? How have they changed life for people living in your state? How have they changed your life?

Collective Reasoning

Directions:

1. Share your findings with the class.

    a. Classmates take notes amendments being shared by peers.

2. After all presenters have gone, answer in writing: what effect has the amendment process had on our state? How have amendments changed life in our state?

Extension Assignment #4: Juries vs. Elections: Different Avenues for Public Influence

Directions on Research Questions: Using the resources available to you, answer the below basic questions about the role of a jury in criminal proceedings.

1. Define "jury"—what are they?
2. In your state, when are defendants entitled to a trial by jury?
3. How are jurors chosen? What might disqualify someone from becoming a juror?

4. How do juries make decisions? What happens if the jury doesn't agree on a judgment?
5. How would you improve the jury process to make it more fair?

Democratic Systems: Comparing Court Proceedings to Election Proceedings

Directions: Compare the ways in which juries and elections offer the public decision-making power. Answer the below questions using what you've learned about juries and elections thus far:

1. Do juries or constituencies make more informed decisions? Explain.
2. Which form of democratic rule (juries or elections) is more prone to abuse? In which system is an unjust, poorly considered outcome more likely?
3. Which institution is MORE democratic? Explain.
4. Should jury procedures look more like election procedures (majority rule, more opportunity for participation regardless of conflict of interest, etc.)? Why or why not?
5. Should election procedures look more like jury procedures? Why or why not?

Note for Instructors: Most students don't seriously study economics until their junior and senior years of high school, and even then the courses tend to be cursory and general. The below two lesson plans are meant for high level students with background knowledge on American history, civics, and government. They are also intentionally brief—they can be turned into homework assignments or added to lessons that focus on the philosophy of Laissez-Faire Capitalism and its relationship to American Liberal Democracy.

At its core, the capitalist logic empowers individuals rather than institutions. By offering individuals the opportunity to become wealthy by creating things that people want, it unlocks human genius and harnesses that genius for social progress. Capitalist societies, because of their decentralized logic and incentive structures, are capable of solving social problems with tremendous speed. Ultimately, capitalism enables individuals to shape the society they want, and creates a more dynamic, ever-changing world. Social renewal through individual empowerment is at the heart of both capitalism and American Liberal Democracy, and the below lessons emphasize this connection. Instructors can, of course, help their students make this connection throughout economics courses as well.

LESSON PLANS: ECONOMICS

Assignment #1: Economics: Creative Destruction in Capitalist Economies

Directions: Read the below description of the concept of "creative destruction," and then answer the associated questions in writing. Prepare to share your responses with the class.

Capitalism is an economic system in which private entities own the means of production and sell what they produce on the free market for profit. Capitalism offers enterprising and talented individuals the freedom to create new things that benefit those around them and then become fabulously wealthy as those people pay them for their products and services. By aligning the interests of the public (for life-improving innovations) with the interests of the private individual (for personal wealth), the capitalist market structure has ushered in a protracted era of intense and widely distributed material prosperity.

Free markets incentivize human inventiveness to the benefit of society as a whole. But as new innovations change how people spend their money, old businesses will die. The horse-drawn carriage industry was decimated by the automobile, and car manufacturers today that don't develop energy efficient vehicles may go the same way. Displacement is an inevitable feature of change, which happens a lot in capitalism. The process by which new innovations transform societies, disrupt life, and make old ways of life obsolete is called *creative destruction*.

1. List the best examples of creative destruction you can think of. Draw on your history (especially American history) courses and your life experiences. Which inventions have been most disruptive for traditional ways of life? Which transformed our societies?
2. Choose one of the examples from #1, and identify the toll of the innovation. How many people lost their jobs? How many businesses were destroyed and how much tax revenue was lost? This will take some research and speculation.

a. For the same event, try to calculate the aggregate benefits to society (jobs gained, fortunes made, stocks driven up, etc.).
   b. Which outweighs the other?

3. Reflect: would you rather live in a society where creative destruction happens nearly continuously or one in which ways of life change much more slowly? Imagine yourself in a society where creative destruction was slowed—how would it be different?
4. Use three adjectives to describe the society in which creative destruction is rapid and frequent, and three adjectives to describe the society in which creative destruction is slow or nonexistent.

Assignment #2: How Do US Political and Economic Values Impact Our Lives?

Directions: Read the text below and answer the associated questions.

Capitalism is an economic system that empowers individuals to buy and sell what they like on the free market with limited government interference. American liberal democracy rests on the political theory, laid out in the Declaration of Independence, that the people are the rightful leaders of the government, which exists to serve them.

Based on the above statements and your background knowledge of capitalism and American democracy, what do these two systems have in common?

Question to Ponder

What effect does emphasis on individual freedom and power have on society as a whole? Both capitalism and American democracy put individuals at the center of society, and expand each of our ability to control our own lives and pursue happiness however we see fit.

Research, and Then Reconsider

Choose a nation that does not have a healthy democracy and strongly capitalist economy, learn about how the lives of their people have changed in the past 30 years. Answer:

1. How has life changed in the past 30 years for the average citizen?

    a. Are the changes for the better? Explain.

2. Who or what drove those changes? Was change driven by the government, corporations, or other groups?
3. How does their type and rate of change compare to the type and rate of change in the US?

Once you've answered the above, answer (in writing and then share to the class):

• How do US and political and economic values influence our lives?

Use your research and knowledge of capitalism and American liberal democracy to answer.

RENEWAL AS A CORE AMERICAN VALUE

The above lesson plans are intended to help students recognize and internalize the third core value of US democracy—in addition to championing *equality* and *freedom*, we're also a nation that prizes *renewal*. Indeed, the long-unsung American value of renewal is easily glimpsed in the never-ending process of interpreting and reinterpreting the principles of equality and freedom. The Civil War was fought over what "equality" and "freedom" should mean in this nation, and the Civil Rights movement 100 years later again revolutionized the national understanding of those words.

Freedom and equality, the principles at the heart of American identity, have evolved profoundly since our founding and continue to change today. Their evolution hasn't originated from on high; it's been driven by the changing beliefs of the public, who—indignant at our national failure to embody our principles—then (eventually) bend policy and legislation to their will. The principle of renewal has been behind the evolution of those other vague (until the public defines them) and powerful values of equality and freedom.

WHY TEACH RENEWAL? A SUMMARY

1. Renewal is energizing. Young people will see that this national value—which is a natural outgrowth of democratic government—is built around them, and that without their input the nation will fail to move forward. They'll come to see elections as opportunities for political renewal and get involved.
2. Renewal is clarifying. It unites themes in American history and highlights features of our governing and economic systems. US and state amendments are artifacts of the value of renewal, and our historical evolution toward a more inclusive and just society is evidence of this principle at work.
3. Renewal is optimistic. It helps young people see our nation as a work in progress, indeed, as a nation that is defined by this process more than any one state. It will encourage soon-to-be citizens to join in the process of renewal, to bring their energy and ideas to civic and political life.

Chapter Three

Teach Democracy as a Way of Life

HELPING STUDENTS PRACTICE COLLECTIVE GOVERNANCE IN THEIR CLASSROOMS AND SCHOOLS

"Democracy is not a state. It is an act, and each generation must do its part to help build what we called the Beloved Community, a nation and world society at peace with itself." —John Lewis

"Democracy is a way of life controlled by a working faith in the possibilities of human nature. Belief in the Common Man is a familiar article in the democratic creed. That belief is without basis and significance save as it means faith in the potentialities of human nature as that nature is exhibited in every human being irrespective of race, color, sex, birth and family, of material or cultural wealth. This faith may be enacted in statutes, but it is only on paper unless it is put in force in the attitudes which human beings display to one another in all the incidents and relations of daily life. To denounce Nazism for intolerance, cruelty and stimulation of hatred amounts to fostering insincerity if, in our personal relations to other persons, if, in our daily walk and conversation, we are moved by racial, color or other class prejudice; indeed, by anything save a generous belief in their possibilities as human beings, a belief which brings with it the need for providing conditions which will enable these capacities to reach fulfillment. The democratic faith in human equality is belief that every human being, independent of the quantity or range of his personal endowment, has the right to equal

opportunity with every other person for development of whatever gifts
he has." —John Dewey, *Democracy and Education*

If democratic societies are defined by the people's capacity to change
them, and especially by younger generations' capacity to align society
and government to their values, then a democratic society expects a lot
of its people. After all, it is not inevitable that every new generation of
Americans will move our nation in a more tolerant, inclusive, delibera-
tive, just direction. What if the next generation rejects our democratic
government and way of life? What if they embrace a partisan identity
that vilifies the beliefs of other Americans? History teaches us that it is
far easier for stable systems to unravel into chaotic, intolerant minority
rule than mature into ones that are defined by peaceful, orderly debate
and compassionate policy.

American citizens simply must buy into the democratic way of life,
and embody democratic norms of public spiritedness, compromise, and
respect for individual dignity as they go about the business of self-
government. Just as the rule of law is a prerequisite for popular renewal, so are widely held democratic norms. If too many of us lack a basic
respect for our fellow citizens' points of view and processes that enable
debate and collective policy making, we will wind up wrecking the
house we all live in.

Democratic renewal through widespread public participation requires a widely shared democratic spirit, which David Foster Wallace
has elegantly described as a disposition that "combines rigor and humility, i.e. passionate conviction plus a sedulous respect for the convic-
tions of other." He goes on: "As any American knows, this is a difficult
spirit to cultivate and maintain, particularly when it comes to issues you
feel strongly about. Equally tough is . . . 100 percent intellectual integrity—you have to be willing to look honestly at yourself and at your
motives for believing what you believe, and to do it more or less continuously." The formidable task of cultivating the type of democratic
character described by John Dewey, David Foster Wallace, and countless others must fall on schools—as the civic institution with the farthest reach in American society and the one explicitly charged with
preparing our young to be positive forces in society.

CIVIC EDUCATION IS MORE ABOUT
CHARACTER THAN CONTENT

Collective governance—especially in a nation with the size and diversity of opinion of the United States—requires a widely distributed democratic skill set. This skill set can be taught, but its most important components aren't so much discrete areas of knowledge or particular talents as they are the habits and mindset that we bring to our interactions with one another. Human psychology is not oriented toward tolerance when faced with strong differences and disagreement, and when our interests are threatened, it's all too easy for the primal part of us to take over, dig in, and fight for survival.

The capacity to disagree productively comes about as a result of training, not impulse. We need to together balance our interests with those of others, which means democratic spirit requires us to displace our deeply laid impulses for survival and replace it with the understanding that long-term prosperity requires respect for the opinions of others, not pursuing short-term interests at any cost.

The same habits that determine whether a dispute on a crowded train will end with fists and resentment or words and understanding are the same ones that enable a nation to engage in protracted—often uncomfortable—dialogue with itself. The same habit that moves some of us to warmly greet grocery store clerks are the same ones that move us to volunteer with nonprofits, join our neighborhood associations, invest time in finding the political candidates who best represent us, and debate differences of opinion with charitable open-mindedness. At its heart, democratic societies operate on a set of values and codes of conduct shared by the vast majority of their citizens.

POLITICS AS ALL-OUT WAR: THE PROBLEM OF VITRIOL IN
AMERICAN PUBLIC LIFE

To be clear, every young person should be taught the theory and mechanics of how our government and economy work, and should be acquainted with how our society has changed throughout American history—knowledge of our national, state, and local institutions is a necessary precondition for active, thoughtful citizenship. But knowledge is not sufficient. We also need to *believe* in the democratic process, and sometimes put it above our own short-term interests. Of course, we must understand the mechanics of our political systems, but we must also be motivated to *use* that understanding to *participate* in those systems with passion and restraint. But if malicious actors use their understanding of political processes to obfuscate, confuse, or distract from the important questions facing our nation, in order to pursue their own particular interests or glorify their own political ideologies, then it harms our collective governing capacity.

Too many Americans today (especially politicians and members of the media) *use* our political processes to advance their own goals in the same way that corporate executives *use* tax law to shield their wealth from being utilized by the rest of us. Those who exploit our legislative system for their own short-term personal gain undermine our free society—they manipulate the letter of the law to subvert its purpose. And they make us all cynics in the process, as those who of us who are willing to concede arguments to opponents and forego personal attacks are seen as weak, uncommitted, or dimwitted. More importantly, when voters, political activists, and representatives restrain themselves from exploiting governing processes in pursuit of short-term policy goals, they tend to lose—outmaneuvered by opponents unburdened by scruples.

No matter how brilliantly designed, checks and balances cannot survive a nation that does not respect them. If elected representatives exploit loopholes in constitutional power for their own personal gain, and become more popular as they do so, our democratic institutions will rot with neglect and eventually act only to rubber stamp presidential edicts. It takes a democratic culture to operate democratic institutions, and schools are our best vehicle for transmitting democratic values to the young. Schools, then, must teach young people democratic habits of mind—which are grounded in an understanding of our government's mechanics but go well beyond mere content knowledge. They have to *practice* self-governance.

POLITICS AS A SIDESHOW: THE PROBLEM OF INDIFFERENCE IN AMERICAN PUBLIC LIFE

Those who choose to opt out of civic and political life do their nation a different type of disservice from those who exploit political processes for short-term gain. Those of us who have learned to say that "politics just isn't my thing," who don't care to learn about the political goings-on in our communities, who don't vote—we've forgotten a part of our identity.

Americans are *both* private individuals who need not justify their behavior to anyone *and* public citizens with formal decision-making power over the rest of us. If we don't utilize that power, we allow our government to be controlled by others. The more people who opt out of participating in politics, the narrower the governing group and the less representative, inclusive, and just our society.

Those who weaponize civic knowledge for their own personal ends betray their own narrow selfishness, but those who choose to not participate in public life altogether fail to recognize their own power and therefore their responsibility to the Americans with whom they share the country. The democratic spirit that schools instill into our young is engaged and magnanimous. It's a spirit that recognizes itself as part of a cherished community of profound significance.

TOCQUEVILLE'S LESSONS TODAY

Public-spiritedness, a strong understanding of American governing structures and political philosophy, the ability to speak in public, research difficult questions, and change your mind when confronted with new information . . . these are the qualities that make for a mature democratic citizen. But the type of advanced citizen with the qualities above is not easily created—the type of restraint and wisdom required for real citizenship is similar to the type required for loving marriages and lifelong friendships. Citizens must be caring yet insistent, demanding yet understanding, inspired yet patient. They must tame their baser human impulses—the ones that drive us to either dominate others or let them do all the work.

Democratic citizenship is in many ways the height of human cultivation, it's the type of moral accomplishment akin to learning how to love selflessly and die with grace. It's a mode of behavior that is deeply civilized, precisely because it runs against primal impulses. Governing as a collective means curbing our deeply human impulses toward behaving as the "ambitious, vindictive, and rapacious" neighbors to which nature predisposes us, to use the three adjectives that James Madison thought encapsulated human nature. That's why civics educators' jobs begin with teaching content and extends to shaping our character.

If democracy is a way of life, civics education must teach the skills and mindsets necessary for leading that life. It's a life that will be defined by balancing compromise and conviction, personal desires with public good. To use the Greek philosopher Aeschylus' phrase, later famously channeled by Bobby Kennedy in a speech after Martin Luther King Jr.'s assassination, civic education is about nothing less than preparing young people to tame "the savageness of man, making gentle the life of this world."

Almost two hundred years ago, Alexis de Tocqueville observed how American "habits of the heart"—a peoples' deeply ingrained behaviors and mindsets—were more democratic than in any other nation he'd encountered. The American people, even in a nation less than fifty years old, had shed the aristocratic tendencies of their British fathers and embraced a culture of free expression, egalitarianism, hard work, and local association. A majority of eligible Americans held public office for some period of time, were members of multiple neighborhood groups (some political and some not), and engaged in frequent, impassioned debates about public policy. All seemed to be engaged in the project of building their towns, which they understood as being part of a larger national project of nation-building.

Americans of the early and mid 1830s, Tocqueville went on to observe, seemed to genuinely relish public life. They attended local political meetings in large numbers, debated politics in bars, and frequently formed groups to advocate for shared concerns. In short, ours was a robust civic culture and deeply democratic way of life. People were invested in one another and understood themselves to be part of national enterprise of considerable importance.

There is no question that the horrors of slavery and the reality of gender inequality stand in sharp contrast to the rosy picture of egalitarian exchange and inclusive civics painted by Tocqueville. But it is worth noting that the glaring hypocrisies of the past no longer exist, having been curbed by centuries of steady legislation (and one horrific war) initiated by Americans who saw these disgraces, objected, and took action.

The power of democracy is in its capacity for self-direction. "We the people" truly are at the helm, and it's the American people—and usually the young ones—who have always driven change in this nation. To continue to do so, we can't merely vote every few years, pay our taxes, and follow the law. It's essential that we live democratic lives. If the next generation is asked to steer a democratic nation without first being steeped in and then learning to embody democratic habits, we put the American experiment at risk.

Successful civic education instills democratic "habits of the heart" into young people. Since democratic habits cannot be taught from a textbook so much as demonstrated and practiced, this section will focus on classroom and whole school strategies that can be applied to myriad social studies topics rather than lesson plans that focus on particular knowledge areas. Next, I propose three democratic habits that schools can and must work to cultivate, and offer tangible, easy-to-implement strategies for doing so.

Part II

Democratic Habits

Chapter Four

Democratic Habit #1

All Citizenship Is Local

BEFRIEND YOUR NEIGHBORS . . . AND YOUR COUNCILMAN (OR AT LEAST TRY)

Do you think of yourself as an individual who happens to live in a national community? Or are you—psychologically—a *member* of that national community? This may seem like a facile question, but how we answer is of enormous national consequence.

In democracies, individuals must also be citizens. What that status means is something worth considering alongside our students. Ultimately, our work as social studies educators must be to help young people integrate "citizen" into their identities—a challenging task given the longstanding American tradition of glorifying individualism and personal freedom.

The scope of democratic citizenship goes far beyond the narrow definition of "citizen" you usually find in dictionaries, which Dictionary.com puts as "a legally recognized inhabitant, subject or national of a state or commonwealth, either native or naturalized." Such definitions fail to communicate the role that "inhabitants" must play in their towns, cities, and "national or state commonwealths." More to the point, they fail to establish the *relationship* between the geographic and political entities and the citizens themselves. That the definition uses the word "subject" betrays its disappointing imprecision. Subjects are charges, not contributors. Citizens are both, possessing rights (endowed by nature and protected by the state) and responsibilities related to steering that state. The definition fails to capture how dependent the state is on its citizens, especially in a democracy.

A definition of "citizen" more fitting for American democracy, one that captures the demands as well as the rights of citizens, is a *self-conscious community member*. A person who knows that they are part of larger whole, and knows that their behavior—good or bad, and whether they like it or not—affects that whole. Those of us who teach US government, economics, and history must make sure that young people take their role as citizen seriously. That starts with persuading them that they *are citizens, not merely individuals, and certainly not subjects*.

To do that we need to attach young people to their communities and help them feel invested in their development. Familiarizing them with democratic theory (through close-readings and discussion of foundational documents) and the structure of US institutions is a crucial piece. Hopefully, they'll develop an attachment to our social and political ideals, especially since those ideals put them at the center of society and make them the most important stakeholders in our system. But the majority of people are not moved to action by a theory—a strong understanding of the principles of American government probably won't inspire many to show up for evening school board meetings or knock on doors for their preferred candidates. But if your child is being bullied at school, or your friend is running for local office, you will show up and advocate for them.

Personal relationships, more than abstract principles, inspire civic action. If young people meet local decision-makers, debate state-level policy questions with invested adults, and intern at a nearby nonprofit, they're going to feel like they're a part of a shared community run through collective governance. They'll see democratic theories brought to life by people and want to join the collective project that is self-government, embodying the noble ideas of collective, inclusive action first penned by our founders and taught by civics teachers ever since. The best way to bring young people into the fold of a democratic society, to engage in the act that is democracy, is to introduce them to somebody who is already doing it.

Former US Speaker of the House Tip O'Neill coined the now-famous phrase "all politics is local," which was likely meant as re-election advice: pay attention to the bread and butter desires of your constituents, not the big symbolic abstractions that tend to consume national politics. Connecting with the people you represent, helping them get a sense of who you are, and reminding them that you know who they are, is just good politics. When constituents feel that they have a personal connection to their representative, even if that connection is as thin as a single handshake years ago, they'll take the time to go to the polls and vote (for you).

Representative O'Neill, who spent thirty years in Congress and ten as Speaker of the House, clearly took his own advice. But his quip was more than merely practical advice for ambitious representatives, it was also a statement on the mechanics of democratic governance. The business of government gets done at evening meetings and in conversation with your neighbors. It's relationships that attach us to our community and move us to contribute to it (through political processes) far more than lofty ideas or cold economic interests.

What is true for politics is also true for citizenship. Those of us who know our child's principal, who chat with local business owners when we enter their shops, and who donate to our neighbors' campaigns for local office develop a unique attachment to our community. When enough people build these connections and develop these attachments, civic culture, which grounded in a basic trust and respect for one another, is born.

Democracy demands collaboration, and collaboration is near impossible without a baseline level of trust. The presumption of goodwill that is at the heart of any real discussion, debate, or negotiation can't be cultivated on social media, that land of anonymous viciousness. It can't be learned by reading the inspired philosophy of our nation's seminal documents. It comes from interactions with the people around us, and rests on the recognition of mutual respect.

SOCIAL TRUST IN NATIONAL POLITICS

At the municipal level, people really can get to know their representatives. They see them in coffee shops, can ask them questions in public meetings, and can stop into their offices. It's even easier to get to know local party, nonprofit, educational, and business leaders—and merely knowing them has the effect of investing us in our community. We know who is in charge and can quickly figure out how to influence them.

But how does this translate to national politics, which takes place in imperious buildings in Washington, DC, carried out by people we will never meet? What does the social trust built by us through interactions at the local level have to do with national policy? Perhaps we can talk through our differences with a neighbor, but why extend the same benefit of the doubt to a stranger thousands of miles away, who lives a life that you'll likely never understand, who probably has no interest in understanding you?

This is an important question and serious critique: national politics happens at the symbolic level—it can't be personal, because nobody can know everyone involved. It's about influencing people you'll never meet and oftentimes will never understand. National politics is about branding, not relationships. This is all true. But the baseline social trust that we develop by engaging in local politics can—and does—translate to the national stage. Social trust is a self-fulfilling prophecy: if I assume that you'll treat me with respect, I'll do the same for you. Operating off of the presumption of mutual decency enables reasonable, open-minded exchange. We must simply will ourselves to trust strangers in other states, who are part of different parties, and who may believe in policies we deem harmful. Doing so means drawing on a reservoir of goodwill built at the local level.

All politics is local, because trust is built locally, at the level of the handshake, eye contact, and small favor. But while social trust is best cultivated by people at the local level who we come to know, it can be applied to the national stage, to those we will never meet. Social trust is about how we regard and treat strangers, not friends. Do we approach others with goodwill, or assume hostility and idiocy from those who aren't like us? The answer to the question of how we treat strangers generally follows from our experiences with our friends, acquaintances, and colleagues. If we've been able to work together with others and accomplish shared goals, talk through differing opinions, and built local networks of mutual dependence, then we'll have developed pro-social mindsets that color our thinking about people across the nation.

And how do our attitudes about one another affect our attitudes about the government? And how does engagement in local politics affect attitudes about American institutions, processes, and leaders? The same formula holds: if we have positive experiences working with government and influencing policy at the local level, the confidence and enthusiasm that such successes engender will be translated to the nation realm. We'll view national politics as a world that is open to our participation and engage.

Social studies teachers must offer students opportunities to join in the civic and political life of their neighborhoods, view such opportunities as a part of their curriculum, and integrate time to do this into the school day. One of the most effective ways of doing so is through civic action projects.

CIVIC ACTION PROJECTS: GOALS AND EXAMPLES

Successful classrooms transport young people out of their four walls and help them fall in love with worlds unknown, and talented teachers can make ancient philosophers and abstract concepts feel like trusted friends. Civics teachers are no different, and the abstraction that we're most focused on bringing to life and helping students feel attached to is the *nation*, and even more importantly, the *American nation*. This can be done in a classroom, but it can be done much more successfully outside of it, where the abstraction manifests in millions of ways.

Shaking the hand of a local representative turns the concept of representative democracy into flesh and bone, and immediately involves you in our grand democratic processes. Perhaps you mention the pothole on your street that has been ruining your tires, ask their thoughts on a recent presidential action, or simply invite them to your Christmas party. When you volunteer with a local food pantry and meet members of your community in need, you begin to develop a relationship with a wider subset of those around you and start to consider their perspective and desires in the course of your daily life.

Such exchanges and acts of service help students develop the mindset of a democratic citizen, a mindset defined by the awareness that we are all interconnected. This is not a spiritual formulation—in democracies, it's literal. As self-governors, we are truly dependent on the decency and engagement of those around us. We simply cannot get by on our own, nor can we depend on political elites to take care of us. We the people are collectively in charge.

Here are some examples of "action-civics" projects and programs that help young people feel rooted in their communities and develop the affection for their fellow citizens that motivates thoughtful, kind, persistent political engagement.

THE CHANGE THE WORLD PROJECT

The mission of Democracy Prep Public Schools is to "educate responsible citizen-scholars for success in the college of their choice and a life of active citizenship." Based in Harlem, the twenty-one-school charter network can be described in much the same way as KIPP or Success Academies—engines of opportunity for low-income students who are ready to work hard and follow the rules. What distinguishes them is their explicitly civic mission, which is exemplified by their Senior Capstone Project, called the Change the World project.

In a year-long course with the same name, each senior takes on a challenge facing their hometown, community, school, nation, or the world at large. They write a research review that describes the history of the problem and offer a theory about its causes. Then they plan a series of actions to help solve it. Actions range from "die-ins" at the local police station to protest police brutality and inapporpriate use of force, to food drives for those in need. At the end of the year, students present their research and impact to a panel of three teachers in something that resembles a PhD thesis defense.

This is a textbook example of action-civics. Students are asked to choose an injustice that they find personally alarming, research it deeply, and then take actions that tangibly help those most affected.

FOUR-STEP FORMULA FOR SUCCESSFUL
CIVIC ACTION PROJECTS

While the Change the World Project has the no-nonsense, high-expectations culture of Democracy Prep stamped onto it, its simple four-step formula can be adapted to nearly any setting (I have personally used this formula in both boutique independent schools and sprawling public schools):

TEXTBOX 4.1

First, students choose a problem that makes them indignant—something that violates their understanding of justice.

To get students thinking about topics, teachers can ask them to:

> Think about a time that you've been angered or saddened by an injustice or by the unfair suffering of another. Consider the times you've felt wronged or known that others were wronged. Write them down—what upset you about what you saw/heard/read?

Younger students will respond better to this type of prompt:

> This is a pitch contest, with an imaginary Bill Gates ready to invest 0ne billion dollars into the best idea here today. He wants to make the world a better place, and will invest in whoever has the best idea for how to do it!

Here are the rules:

1. Identify an issue / problem you see in the world. Describe it.
2. Propose a solution
3. Convince Bill Gates to invest $1B in your solution

This is a Pitch Contest. You may use:

- Words
- Images
- Videos

Winning pitches will convince us that your issue is important and that you have a creative, viable solution.

There will be students, especially in younger grades, who simply cannot think of a problem with the world, or at least not one that they want anything to do with. There are a few simple ways to offer these students avenues into understanding and seeing the significance of large-scale social problems.

Teachers can help students choose the topic by:

1. Asking them to consider the content they've learned in other classes—what have the books they've read in English, the accounts they've heard of our history, and the conclusions of their science teachers, that they find wrong? After reviewing their notes, can they truly find no alarm bells about our world today?

2. Showing students the UN's Sustainable Development Goals (SDGs) graphic and descriptions, which organizes our world's modern challenges into seventeen categories, from "Poverty" to "Affordable and Clean Energy" to "Quality Education." Teachers can then ask students to find, through their own experiences or research, their own examples of each challenge. Where do these categories show up in their lives, and around the world?

3. Summarize John Rawls' "veil of ignorance" theory of justice, which says that a perfectly fair society would be one in which residents are blind to their own socio-economic status as they develop their political ideologies and policy preferences. If lawmakers were also subject to Rawl's "veil of ignorance," they'd be unable to use their position to benefit themselves and those like them—they will be incentivized to create a society that maximizes benefits for every type of person, since they could be any type of person.

   Of course, our lawmakers do know how laws will affect them, meaning that we probably do not live in a totally fair society. If our lawmakers DID make laws behind the "veil of ignorance," how would the world be different?

   a. a.When students offer their answers, teachers tell them to use their analysis as basis for choosing their topics. Choose the most egregious disparity they find, or the one that they find most offensive.

Past students have chosen (among thousands of others):

1. Climate change gentrification
2. Normalizing conversations about depression for men
3. Reducing gun violence in low-income neighborhoods
4. Addressing the global water crisis
5. Housing insecurity in Miami Dade County

Topics can be phrased in terms of the problem (e.g., Climate change gentrification) or solution (e.g., Addressing the global water crisis), and with them a brief description of why the student chose the topic—what makes it a problem worth trying to solve?

TEXTBOX 4.2

Second, students engage in deep research on the topic.

The more we learn about something, the more invested we tend to become in it and the more capable we become of developing creative solutions.

Students are next required to build their understanding of the problem they've chosen. They're charged with identifying the origins of the injustice they've focused on and the understanding the forces that continue to feed it today. Research can be done through interviews with subject experts, policy-makers, or those most affected by the problem. They can also include a literature review that teaches the basics of academic research. The most elemental version could simply require students to find 2–5 articles / experts on the issue and then summarize their theories on the causes and consequences of the problem.

Teachers can use the following assignments to help students see the power and value of deep research before taking action:

1. "There are a thousand hacking at the branches of evil to one who is striking at the root." —Henry David Thoreau

    a. Interpret the above quote in your own words. What is Thoreau's point? Which strategy is more effective for removing evil—"hacking at the branches" or "striking at the root"? Explain.
    b. Offer an example of an initiative that is "hacking at the branches of evil."
    c. Now share an example of one that is "striking at the root."
    d. Explain the difference between the two initiatives.

2. Initial Hypothesis Search: offer your educated guess for WHY your problem exists. What is the driving force that continues to make your problem a problem? Why does the problem simply solve itself? What's standing in the way?

a. Offer 3–5 hypotheses for the CAUSE of your problem.
b. Share your hypotheses with the class. The class offers
   feedback—which one sounds like the most likely?
c. Identify your next steps: what research will you have
   to do to either substantiate or disprove your hypothesis? Create a "research plan" in which you lay out your
   next steps.

TEXTBOX 4.3

Third, take action to help those in need.

Depending on the grade level and timeline, student actions can include things as simple as creating a social media page that makes others
aware of the problem. Other teachers and school leaders might require
actions that have a tangible, measurable impact on those most affected.
For example, students might be expected to intern at an organization
that is working to solve the problem they've chosen or lead a food drive
and donate the proceeds directly to those in need.

TYPES OF ACTIONS

1. Fundraisers for local organizations working to solve the student's chosen problem

   a. For example, students might put on a bake sale and
      donate the proceeds to a food pantry, animal shelter, or
      environmental group.

2. One-time direct service activity

   a. For example, spending a Saturday picking litter up
      from a local park.
   b. Extension: group one-time service activity. A student-
      leader organizes a group of her peers to pre-register
      teenagers to vote.

3. Recurring service activity, through an existing organization

    a. Extension: the student could start a service-internship, in which they work for organizations that need their help.

    b. Extension Extension: the student could organize a group of peers to do service-internships at a local organization.

4. Recurring student-lead service activity

    a. Students could identify a novel service activity and invest their peers in pursuing it regularly.

    b. For example, during the COVID-19 pandemic, students created a "Digital Tutoring Network" in Miami, which connected elementary students in need of homework help with high school students willing to tutor them.

5. Service-Advocacy: persuade elected officials to take action to solve their problem

    a. For example, students have gone to city council meetings to persuade them to adopt or support legislative on issues ranging from the gender pay gap to human trafficking.

TEXTBOX 4.4

Fourth, describe their process and impact to a group of stakeholders.

After playing the role of scholar and activist—engaging in deep research about the causes and consequences of their social problem and then taking action to help those most affected—students must finally account for their work, reflect on their impact, and improve their strategies.

There are various ways for students to share, brag about, defend, and grow from their work. Here are some ways that schools structure this final leg of the civic-action project:

1. A Civics Fair!

   a. Students can create posters that summarize their work and prepare talking points for interested parties.
   b. This strategy works best when an entire school or grade launch civic-action projects in tandem. But they can be effective even in the context of a class.
   c. School leaders and teachers could invite the larger community to the fair, asking teachers, parents, community partners, and members of the larger community to attend.

2. An Impact Defense

   a. This is a more formal, scholarly exercise modeled after a PhD Thesis Defense, in which students present the results of their research, the actions they took based on that research, and the tangible impact of those actions.
   b. For the sake of increased rigor, students should present to a small panel (3–9) of teachers, administrators, and community members with expertise on the students' topic. So, if the topic is related to the effects of sea level rise in South Florida, the panel might include the AP environmental science teacher, an employee of a local nonprofit that's committed to reducing the effects of sea level rise, and a student with a similar topic.

3. A Showcase

   a. A celebratory event that highlights exemplary student work. Students are chosen for the Showcase based on the depth of their impact and commitment, and are given the opportunity to share their work with an audience composed of members of the local community, parents, school faculty and staff, and their peers.

b. The showcase format incentivizes students by turning it into a competition—students will be competing for slots in the Showcase. Showcases bring attention to student impact, which can help service work become a mark of prestige within the school, and positively impact school culture.

Chapter Five

Democratic Habit #2

Facilitating Productive Disagreements

Rauch pointed out that every society has an epistemic regime, a market-place of ideas where people collectively hammer out what's real. In democratic, nontheocratic societies, this regime is a decentralized eco-system of academics, clergy members, teachers, journalists and others who disagree about a lot but agree on a shared system of rules for weighing evidence and building knowledge. —David Brooks

At the core of citizenship is the recognition that we are in this together. We are equal members of a beloved community—as such, we need to understand each other. To do that, we need to listen carefully, respond thoughtfully, listen again, and repeat.

At their best, democracies are chaotic and colorful manifestations of the scientific process. They're a national bazaar of ideas, opinions, platforms, and demands—all in perpetual contact and conflict, always refining each other. A deeply diverse, educated nation that is commit-ted to freedom of expression sounds poised for important, mutually edifying debates that yield deftly innovative policy solutions to intract-able problems. American democracy should be the scientific process on steroids, and our collective debate should have yielded a nearly perfect society by now!

But rather than refining each others' ideas with healthy competition, we tend to focus on annihilation. Political debates too frequently morph into take-no-prisoner verbal assaults that aim to vilify the opponent rather than surface new insights. Politicians, pundits, and millions of American citizens appear to have already decided what they believe, and have no interest in engaging in anything other than attack with those who disagree with them.

When political speech comes to be seen as a weapon, exchange is lost. Because real exchange demands genuine curiosity, and curiosity is born from the recognition that *you don't know everything.* The near wholesale abandonment of open-mindedness in mainstream political discourse is alarming in a nation that claims to be the greatest democracy on earth. What is exchange without the willingness to change your mind? And what is democracy without exchange?

For civic discourse to mean anything, it must be grounded on that most basic of intellectual foundations: doubt. Socrates' famous formulation—that he knows that he knows nothing, and that is the basis of his wisdom—has been discarded and replaced with a blithe confidence in our belief systems and vitriolic disdain for those with different ideas. This sort of anti-intellectualism harms any individual who subscribes to it—making them abandon inquiry and stunting their development—but in democracies, it also has widespread social consequences. Representatives who know that their constituents will not reward meaningful debate or compromise will begin to approach their political rivals as enemies rather than colleagues, and consider any means of stymieing them a victory.

A climate in which our representatives adopt warlike stances against those with different political beliefs and come to view dominance rather than exchange as the mandate of their constituents will yield a government that is gridlocked during crises, promotes arguments untethered to facts, and ultimately fails to move the nation forward.

As the people go, so go their leaders. Today, American political culture is weakened by dogma and antagonism, but it's still strong enough to shape the behavior of our representatives, who are driven by personal ambition to please us. In the United States, our leaders take their cues from us, the people. In schools, young people take their cues from us, their teachers.

It's our job to teach them to value inquiry, develop intellectual humility, and seek to engage meaningfully with those who hold opposing worldviews. It's no exaggeration to say that the promise of our democracy depends on the next generation mastering the art of productive disagreement and holding their leaders to higher standards of exchange.

What follows is a series of strategies that civics educators can use to teach students the habit of productive disagreement and inculcate the open-mindedness that underlies all mutually instructive discussions and debates. The first rule of this book was to teach US history, government, and economics as debatable subjects whose meaning is ever-evolving and subject to perennial interpretation and argument. Here, I describe strategies for teaching the skills young people need to engage in meaningful debate and dialogue. By explicitly teaching these skills, teachers set students up to participate in the ongoing debates over what to make of our history and how to improve our governing and economic systems. Socratic seminars are a potent tool for teaching the central activity in healthy democracies: meaningful exchange.

SOCRATIC SEMINARS: BUILDING THE HABIT OF CIVIL DISCOURSE

The principles of Socratic Seminars in social studies:

1. Students are presented with philosophical questions about society that lack empirically correct answers. The best questions will draw on timeless American political debates and foundational documents, be related to current events, and relate to recently learned course concepts.
2. Students are given resources (essays, documentaries, songs, etc.) that contextualize the question. Ideally, teachers offer Socratic questions that are directly related to material the students had recently studied.
3. Teacher gives a writing assignment due the day of the Socratic Seminar that asks students to answer all of or part of the question they will discuss that day. Teachers collect and grade these assignments.
4. Teachers share the rules and goals of the seminar and provide students with a rubric clearly explaining what is expected of them and how their participation will translate into a grade.

    a. The goal is to uncover new insights by challenging and building on each others' ideas. This is not about YOU winning, this is about us learning. Challenge

your classmates to get closer to the truth, not to "own" them.
   b. Step up, step back. Everyone must contribute, and nobody can dominate. Encourage your peers who haven't yet shared to offer their thoughts.
   c. Reference evidence whenever possible. When it's not possible, share that.

   a. Please take intellectual risks! Feel free to offer your own thoughts on these important questions—just separate your conjectures from evidence-based points.

5. Students reflect on their performance and takeaways after the seminar. Students can:

   a. Rate themselves according to a simple rubric that is based on the rules and goals of the seminar.
   b. Set goals for the next Socratic Seminar. What can they do better next time?
   c. Record whether their minds were changed by the discussion. What points did their peers surface that they hadn't yet considered?

NOTES ON SOCRATIC SEMINARS

The above structure is intentionally general and meant to be adapted to a wide range of learning environments. Teachers might use Socratic Seminars as end-of-term assessments or more frequently, as vehicles for student discussion. For large classes (more than twenty), teachers might break students into two groups. One group sits in a circle outside the Socratic Seminar circle, observing the discussion and taking notes. Then, groups switch roles. Teachers might participate in the seminars—offering a model for how to participate—or act as note-takers, forcing students to step up and lead the group in new directions when there is a lull. There are many ways to structure Socratic Seminars, but those that are designed to build democratic culture must include:

1. A requirement that all students participate.

2. The expectation that students will be actively listening, referencing their peers' ideas when offering their own thoughts, and attempting to understand the source of disagreements when they arise.

3. Challenging social questions that are relevant to students lives and rooted in social philosophy. Research should help students answer the questions, but not be able to PROVIDE the answers. It's best to have sub-questions within the larger question that are more tangible and give students something to grab onto as they grapple with the larger, more challenging and abstract question. Example questions might include:

    a. Was the American Civil War inevitable?

        a. What was the most important cause of the Civil War?
        b. What actions did Americans attempt to avoid war?
        c. Could the founding fathers—in forging a Constitution in 1789—have anticipated the Civil War and taken actions to prevent it?

    b. To what extent has the United States lived up to its promise to provide equality and freedom for all?

        a. Define "equality" and "freedom"—what does a nation that is truly free and equal look like?
        b. Do equality and freedom always come together, or are they opposed to each other somehow?
        c. Are some groups in the United States "more free" than others? How so?

    c. When, if ever, should the government intervene in the economy? Why?

        a. Is it the government's job to alleviate poverty?
        b. Is it the government's job to guarantee our happiness?
        c. Is it efficient for the government to intervene in the economy? Define "efficient."

    d. Has the American Dream been pursued at the expense
       of African Americans?

         a. What is the American Dream? Define it.
         b. Are you living the American Dream? If so, what
           enables that? If not, what's holding you back?
         c. What has held African Americans back from pur-
           suing the American Dream?

    e. Should the United States promote liberal democracy
       abroad?

         a. What is liberal democracy? Define it.
         b. What do we mean by "promote"? Define it.
         c. Is liberal democracy the best form of government
           available to mankind? Explain.

Note: There are hundreds more potential topics, and a rich place to find many of them is by combing through the National Speech and Debate Association's Lincoln-Douglas Debate Resolutions. While they're framed as statements, they address timeless and profound social questions that American citizens would do well to grapple with. They serve as excellent introductions to the principles of democratic societies and the unresolved debates within them, and help students feel a part of these debates.

    The goals of Socratic Seminars are no more and no less than to teach young people how to interact like democratic citizens—how to identify disagreement on issues that affect us all, and then work those issues out without bitterness, condescension, or resentment. As aspiring democratic citizens ourselves, we all know that actually doing this is extraordinarily difficult. David Foster Wallace, the great writer and political scientist, described the burden of citizenship with characteristic force and clarity:

> A Democratic Spirit is one that *combines rigor and humility*, i.e. passionate conviction plus a sedulous respect for the convictions of others. As any American knows, this is a difficult spirit to cultivate and maintain, particularly when it comes to issues you feel strongly about. Equally tough is a DS's criterion of 100 percent intellectual integrity—you have to be willing to *look honestly at yourself and at your motives* for believing what you believe, and to do it more or less continually.

This kind of stuff is advanced US citizenship. A true Democratic Spirit is up there with religious faith and emotional maturity . . . qualities that people spend their whole lives working on. A Democratic Spirit's constituent *rigor and humility* and *self-honesty* are, in fact, so hard to maintain on certain issues that it's almost irresistibly tempting to fall in with some established dogmatic camp and to follow that camp's line on the issue and let your position harden within the camp and become inflexible and to believe that the other camps are either evil or insane and to spend all your time and energy trying to shout over them. (emphasis author's own)

But perhaps *quality* is too flippant and narrow a word for traits that underpin our democratic society. Socratic Seminars help students build *virtue*, which are individual qualities that create pro-social outcomes. Virtuous citizens are the lifeblood of healthy democracies.

If we were to reward leaders who treat one another with empathy and engage in policy making that is grounded in evidence and punish leaders who stoke antipathy and ignore policy experts, our representatives would quickly get the message and change their behavior. Instilling democratic habits in young people and teaching them to expect their representative to display those values, then, must be the chief priority of civic education. And the only way to learn new habits is to practice them. Socratic seminars are one form of practice—below are some others.

THE NATIONAL SPEECH AND DEBATE ASSOCIATION: THE PROGRAM FOR CREATING CITIZEN-INTELLECTUALS

The National Speech and Debate Association is an American treasure. They've been quietly building a national school subculture that this fiercely committed to intellectual exchange, evidence-based argument, open-mindedness, and student-leadership for decades. Debate Clubs throughout America—and their well-attended weekend tournaments, enervating twelve-hour marathons that they are—are bastions of civic energy.

Their rules can be byzantine and disorienting numerous, but they ultimately orient young people toward the end goal of all serious debates: insight. While victory is rewarded and celebrated, those who hope to be victors must treat their opponents with courtesy and restraint, make arguments that are grounded in fact and analysis, and be capable of changing their positions at a moment's notice. The National

Speech and Debate Association has created a culture and competitive structure that honors ideas and discourages deflection and personal attacks. They use the weighty incentives of shiny trophies and college scholarships to teach young people that meaningful exchanges are fact-based, responsive to counter-points, and mutually instructive. While any school would benefit from participating in the National Speech and Debate Association's competitions, it's also rather simple to recreate their processes in-house. Following are the essential components of a debate program that teaches advanced democratic citizenship.

THREE-STEP FORMULA FOR CIVIL AND RIGOROUS DEBATE (WITH EXAMPLE TOPICS)

First

Students grapple with challenging moral questions about how people ought to treat one another. The most important questions in the social sciences address morality, and consider the roots of human happiness and the interplay between culture and human nature. They should be questions that students will consider and reconsider throughout their lives—they will not be resolved in the class, because they have no open-and-shut resolution. They are the types of questions that prompt lifelong internal evaluation and push adolescents and adults to continuously reevaluate their own political ideologies.

When young people grapple with difficult, foundational questions about how the government should treat its citizens, how citizens should treat their government, and what Americans—bound together by a shared nation—all owe each other and the rest of the world, they develop the intellectual humility and deep curiosity necessary to debate others in good faith.

Second

They force students to change their positions on the same question and argue on behalf of perspectives with which they disagree. Certainty is the enemy of a free society—it stifles dialogue, mutes empathy, and nips individual and collective growth in the bud. It enables the type of intellectual arrogance that stops thinking in its tracks, and ultimately renders us stupid, stubborn, and committed to causes we don't fully understand. Successful debate programs leave students with a convincible mind, and an eagerness to refine their ideas in the fires of debate.

Third

They make the purpose of debate clear: insight. Victory is ancillary to learning, because the issues under debate are more important than any trophy, grade, or feather in the cap.

Below are some past resolutions from the Speech and Debate Association's Lincoln Douglas tournaments, the debate style that explicitly focuses students' attention on long-debated topics in democratic theory. They tend to be deeply engaging for high school students, and can be reworded to help middle school students better grasp their import:

1. Civil disobedience in a democracy is morally justified
2. The United States ought to guarantee universal childcare
3. The United States ought not provide military aid to authoritarian regimes
4. The United States ought to guarantee the right to housing
5. The United States ought to promote democracy in the Middle East

The above are merely a sampling amid hundreds more powerful topics.

Advanced citizens are both activists and intellectuals—they see disagreements as opportunities to both persuade and learn. They recognize that the close-minded activist may well be fighting for a cause they don't fully understand, and that armchair intellectuals could have thought their way into beliefs that are functionally useless. To combine the skepticism of the scientist with the zeal of a change-maker is hard work. It takes time. But it's what robust democracy requires, and like anything else, practice helps, and the younger one starts the easier it becomes.

Chapter Six

Democratic Habit #3

A Middle Path Between Polarization and Indifference

The American identity is wrapped up in lofty and beautiful princi-ples—the sanctity of the individual, economic and political freedom, a commitment to equality, self-government, and generational renewal—that young people must understand and feel connected to. That connec-tion cannot be grounded in excess optimism or blithe deception—they need to understand that these principles have always been aspirations, and our nation has never succeeded in fully embodying them. Not even today. But we have progressed toward more fully realizing those prin-ciples, and they continue to serve as guides for every new generation taking up the mantle of American self-government.

Teaching young people the content of US government and history is a crucial aspect of training them as competent citizens, but ideas only have so much staying power. To really teach the practice of democratic citizenship, young people need to *practice it.* To help students *live* the challenges and thrills of collective governance, educators can create school structures that mirror democratic institutions. In working within those structures, students will develop habits of citizenship. School designs that discourage student input, de-incentivize collective deci-sion-making and compromise, and treat students as wards rather than collaborators will instill a sense of helplessness and indifference that undermines school cultures and slowly kills democracies.

Democratic societies—like so much else—are self-fulfilling prophecies. If the majority of citizens believe themselves capable of living the rigors of self-government, then they will take the actions necessary to participate. Unsurprisingly, people who are accustomed to achieving their goals and relying on others tend to vote in far higher rates than those who believe that they lack the ability to change their circumstances and who subscribe to a cynical view of the world.

One's belief in their own personal efficacy has a direct effect on the extent and nature of their political participation. Those of us who believe ourselves capable of creating positive outcomes in our own lives tend to take the same approach to society. We attempt to influence our communities at large, and even if we don't succeed, we try again. And again. And when it comes to democracies, it's the attempts that really matter. Our free and open societies can abide a wide range of policies, but they wither in the face of popular indifference and their institutions become hollowed out with neglect.

Involving young people in school governance teaches them that they can change their surroundings, and that their ideas matter. Schools and classrooms can teach civics by creating and promoting avenues for student participation—linkage institutions that connect students to the machinations of school governance, to use a favorite term of AP government curricula. Student governments, newspapers, and clubs, and student-influenced disciplinary systems give young people some control and responsibility over their environment, and nothing prompts action and grows maturity like responsibility and power.

When the processes by which schools are administered are porous, transparent, and strongly influenced by its students (the majority of the school's population and their most important stakeholders), then young people learn the standards and skills of democratic governance as matters of course, and will begin to embody democratic habits unthinkingly. Government textbooks and courses will exist to formalize rather than reveal the structures, theories, and lifestyles that come with a democratic way of life, and young people will have practiced the art of living as self-governors of their schools before graduating into self-governors of their towns, states, and nation. They will have seen their actions affect formal policy, learned how citizens can best navigate shared governing structures, and lived that essential lesson: *collective progress depends on individual action, and they are the individuals who must lead.*

THE DANGERS OF PARTISANSHIP

Whether we participate in our government matters a great deal, but *how* we participate may matter even more. Perhaps we believe ourselves capable of affecting communal change, and fear the same of those who hold divergent policy views. To stop them from using government to turn our lives upside down, we vilify and marginalize, we shut them down and shut them up, and assume a war-like posture toward their every action.

There are few emotions more energizing than fear and hatred, and when we feel this way about our fellow citizens—those whose attitudes might be translated into policies that materially alter our lives—we take action. When large segments of a democratic society believe that the other segment is out to get them, then the discourse necessary for broadly beneficial policy-outcomes breaks down. Conversation degrades into verbal battle, and the essential competition of ideas that yields shared insights is replaced by disparaging accusations and outlandish assertions.

Political actors, ever attentive to the public's ever-shifting sensibilities, will respond to partisan contempt with more of the same. They will adopt the histrionic language of political battle, painting their allies as patriots seeking to restore a nation under assault and their opponents as spineless traitors feverishly seeking to turn our nation into something grotesque and alien. They will pitch themselves as national saviors fighting to dispel the enemies in our midst. New political actors will arise, with public identities crafted to channel the partisan antipathy of the moment. They will proudly shun compromise and declare longstanding norms of political cooperation traitorous and duplicitous—mere traps that the partisan enemies have long used to gain power. Recognizing the electoral benefits of a deeply partisan constituency (intensity of partisan identity is directly correlated with voting likelihood), representatives will go from *using* to *stoking* public division.

This might create a vicious cycle of deepening hatred between Americans, as partisan identifications become more extreme and we become increasingly intolerant of those with opposing views. Eventually, partisan contempt seeps into our personal relationships, our friend circles become politically homogenous, and family members with different party affiliations slowly transform into strangers. Sound familiar?

If the chief goal of civic education is to invest young people in our national community, then widespread partisanship is an indication of failure. Partisans are invested in a portion of the nation, and mistake the rest of it for their enemy. As civic educators, it's our job to invest young people in our entire national project, and teach them how to use political parties to organize their thinking and connect with the state. Political parties are neither tools for annihilation nor holy organizations in possession of immutable truths—they are simply vehicles that help an enormous and staggeringly diverse nation organize its political disagreements. With a population already in the throes of an ongoing partisan war, it's all too easy for civics teachers and school administrators to inflame rather than analyze our national differences, and it's essential that we avoid doing so.

When political participation is motivated by vitriol, the free exchange of ideas that is the lifeblood of democratic societies wanes, political opponents come to view one another as enemies playing a zero-sum game, and common ground becomes invisible. If a state of stifled dialogue and deep distrust persists for too long, sectional loyalties can overtake national ones, and political actors may justify undermining national goals in pursuit of party goals.

In the United States, we've seen how a culture of political sectionalism can undermine the long-established democratic norms of cooperation that enable policy-making. Consider how the Supreme Court nomination process has changed from a largely staid procedure of checking a nominee's legal qualifications into a dramatic and ruthless partisan battle with each party hell-bent on getting their judges onto the top bench for life.

The Republican and Democratic Parties have increasingly adopted a scorched-earth style of politics, apparently forgetting that we all stand on the same earth after the battle is over. But "hard-ball" politics—the type that eschew basic norms of inter-party cooperation and basically treats members of the other party as suspects and enemies instead of rivals and thought-partners—tends to clock wins in the short term. Mitch McConnell successfully blocked Merrick Garland, President Obama's Supreme Court nominee, by arguing that a lame duck president should defer to the newly elected president when a Supreme Court seat opens up. After all, new presidents have been freshly approved by the American people, and therefore have the right to make such an important decision.

In precisely the same circumstance in 2020, but this time with republican President Donald Trump as the lame duck, McConnell sped the outgoing president's Supreme Court nominee through the Senate in two weeks. Together with Donald Trump, Mitch McConnell seated three new Supreme Court Justices in eight years (a four-seat swing, considering Garland's denial) and filled 40 percent of the federal judiciary with conservative judges, all now serving lifetime appointments. Leader McConnell won. At least according to his fellow Republicans, among whom he is extremely popular because of his cutthroat effectiveness in pursuing conservative policy goals.

Many Democrats, justifiably indignant and enraged, have responded with plans to expand the Supreme Court when they next control both the executive and legislative branches and pack the new seats with liberal judges. While not unconstitutional, such an action could turn the judiciary into a political pawn—perhaps the Republicans should expand the court further the next time they hold congress and the presidency? And then when the Democrats eventually get them both back, why shouldn't they increase them again? In fifty years, maybe we'll have twenty-five SCOTUS justices, or maybe fifty or a hundred.

Those who believe that party goals are more important than national goals, or that they are one and the same as national goals, may be able to justify subordinating the judicial branch—which is meant to be the great stalwart against the capriciousness of the majority and stolidly uphold the rule of law without fear or favor—to partisan interests. If partisan goals are more important than national ones, maybe turning every annual budget into a crisis that may shut down the government if xyz provision isn't included can be justified. While we don't have time here to list every instance in which partisanship has undermined orderly and effective government, suffice it to say that it happens often. In short, partisan brinkmanship may win the day for the party, but it risks the long-term health of the nation and turns us into cynics in the meantime.

CONSIDERING A COUNTER ARGUMENT: CONFRONTATION'S ROLE IN CHANGE

Power concedes nothing without a demand. It never did and it never will. Find out just what any people will quietly submit to and you have found out the exact measure of injustice and wrong which will be imposed upon them, and these will continue till they are resisted with

either words or blows, or with both. The limits of tyrants are prescribed
by the endurance of those whom they oppress. —Frederick Douglass

My case for teaching young people to shed partisan rancor and revere
democratic institutions and norms may sound idealistic to some and
offensively tone-deaf to others. After all, American history shows us
that meaningful social change nearly always results from tense, uncom-
promising confrontation, and that the "longstanding norms of cooperation" that I argue we should be teaching young people to revere did an
excellent job of protecting the institution of slavery for centuries, disen-
franchised women for longer, and continues to succeed in entrenching
the power of the wealthy, well connected, and white. In modern times,
the democratic processes I so fulsomely praised have allowed us to
remain enmeshed in disastrous foreign wars and have exacerbated economic inequality, to name just a few unsavory policies.

Moreover, history shows us that leaps in social progress are usually
less about fair-minded compromise and more the result of one side
digging in and refusing to accept defeat. Progress usually begins with
broken norms and ends with hurt feelings. It's ushered in by visionaries
willing to go against the grain of settled social conventions, animated
by a thirst for justice. Moderates seeking consensus and prioritizing
politeness usually don't get much done.

Reverend Martin Luther King Jr. immortalized the critique of moderation in the pursuit of justice and social progress in his famous "Letter from a Birmingham Jail," which is worth quoting at length here:

> First, I must confess that over the last few years I have been gravely
> disappointed with the white moderate. I have almost reached the regret-
> table conclusion that the Negro's great stumbling block in the stride
> toward freedom is not the White Citizen's Council-er or the Ku Klux
> Klanner, but the white moderate who is more devoted to "order than to
> justice; who prefers a negative peace which is the absence of tension to
> a positive peace which is the presence of justice; who constantly says "I
> agree with you in the goal you seek, but I can't agree with your methods
> of direct action;" who paternalistically feels he can set the timetable for
> another man's freedom; who lives by the myth of time and who con-
> stantly advises the Negro to wait until a "more convenient season."
>
> Shallow understanding from people of goodwill is more frustrating
> than absolute misunderstanding from people of ill will. Lukewarm ac-
> ceptance is much more bewildering than outright rejection.

King was addressing white moderates who were urging he and his allies to forego acts of civil disobedience and instead pursue their racial justice goals without breaking any existing laws. But that process had repeatedly rebuffed King's efforts. He and other leaders of the Civil Rights Movement had spent years writing letters to members of Congress and State Houses, frequently sought audiences with governors, and vigorously supported the elections of sympathetic politicians in the South. Nothing had worked. Policy-making processes appeared calcified, intent on icing out voices of reform. It would have been an insult to the cause of civil rights to throw up their hands and declare that cause dead because it had failed to be absorbed by our conventional democratic processes. King argued that our democratic processes—not the goals of the Civil Rights Movement—were to blame. He was right.

When democratic processes obstruct rather than facilitate progress, shouldn't we change the process rather than abandon progress? The answer from both parties appears to be a resounding "yes." The huge problem, the one, dear reader, that you've already anticipated is that *the parties disagree on what constitutes progress.* Complicating things further is the fact that *they always have.* So, when overriding democratic norms in the name of progress becomes acceptable is a matter of apparently irreconcilable disagreement. Most of us can agree that some causes (i.e., Civil Rights) are important enough to justify radically changing institutional norms and settled procedures, but few of us can come to a consensus on the causes. Which piece of legislation is important enough to eliminate the filibuster? What line must the Republicans cross before Democrats feel justified in packing the courts? What circumstances would justify members of Congress voting to decertify a popular election?

Political debates will always be intense in this country, and lots of people will always be passionate about lots of issues. And on the question of which issues are more important than maintaining functional, orderly democratic institutions and the rule of law, we mostly disagree. American history is replete with examples of institutions blocking necessary progress and examples of individuals and groups violating norms and laws to advance noble causes.

It took riots in 1968 to push the Democratic Party—and the Republican Party shortly after—to allow voters rather than party insiders to choose their presidential candidates. It was civil disobedience and defiant, indignant rhetoric that created the conditions necessary to pass the 1964 Civil Rights Act. Further back, it was war—and not conventional politics—that eradicated the evil of slavery. Leaps in progress are usually accompanied by unconventional, norm-shattering behavior. And while we can all agree that pursuing justice can indeed sometimes be more important than order, it's also clear that it can't *always be.*

American citizens, in short, must be both devoted to advancing justice and equality while also being committed to preserving and strengthening the democratic processes that tend to put the brakes on sweeping, immediate change. Our government is designed to force deliberation and compromise, and to discourage rapid reforms that are often reactionary and could inspire equally rapid back-swings. Balancing people-driven change with institutional stability is a core goal of democratic governments, and citizens should be taught to hold both priorities in mind simultaneously.

As they pursue turning their political beliefs into law, the American citizen must also prize institutional integrity, and work to strengthen the processes that enable us all to continue to peacefully influence government. This is hard, to say that it requires discipline would be an understatement. The willingness to put institutional process above political issues we care deeply about requires *sustained restraint in service of a larger purpose.* Citizenship implies a public spiritedness that runs against the grain of American individualism, it orients us toward goals that are larger than ourselves and essentially shared. It's public spiritedness that stops us from tearing down the house when we don't get our way and is the essential bulwark against the harmful partisan politics that advocate for doing just that.

When students are treated as partners in school governance, they will learn how to promote their interests while also respecting the interests of others, identifying the common ground upon which action can be taken, and prioritizing the growth of the school community over their personal preferences. They'll learn the skills necessary for shared leadership and leave school ready to help lead that most fractious and unwieldy of communities: our country.

So, which policy priorities justify breaking institutional norms? Thankfully, K–12 civics educators need not answer this question. We should, however, present it. One better, let's give our students the opportunity to live these questions by putting them at the helm.

EXAMPLES OF SCHOOL STRUCTURES THAT TEACH DEMOCRATIC CITIZENSHIP

Democracies wither and rot when their populations are indifferent to public life, and are torn apart participation in public life is motivated by hate, contempt, and fear of their national neighbors. Schools, charged with shaping young people into the democratic citizens upon which free societies draw their strength and dynamism, must help them feel both efficacious and open-minded, empowered enough to lead and humble enough to listen. We must instill a sense of reverence into the hearts of young people: reverence for the shared norms of cooperation that enable democratic governments to be both responsive to the people and institutionally stable.

Politicians, who have learned that they can become famous by exploiting partisan antagonism and whipping up anger, have proved themselves to be unreliable advocates of democratic institutions. It's educators, charged with shaping the perspectives of young citizens, who have the harder job of teaching the young to place the passions of the moment in the context of the larger democratic project, and teach them the art of pursuing justice while strengthening rather than degrading the processes that will enable others to continue that pursuit into the future.

Part III

Democratizing School Structures

Chapter Seven

Practicing Citizenship Strategy #1

Participatory Budgeting

"The budget is the strategy," said a Biden staffer when a reporter asked the administration to clarify its policy priorities. Budgets generally are. A sloppily assembled or nonexistent budget demonstrates a lack of strategy and priorities, and a meticulous one is a roadmap to its assembler's values and goals. Those charged with creating balanced budgets can't speak in hyperbole or support every cause that incites their passions—they have to make hard decisions about who gets what, and know their decisions will kill important projects and hurt people in need.

The old adage that every American wants more government services and lower taxes would evaporate into irrelevance if we were all asked to stare down the barrel of our national, state, and local budgets. As is, we elect others to do that inglorious and tedious work for us, and then criticize their heartlessness and stupidity from afar. Generally, regular voters who don't hold elected office know that the government has a large budget, that the work of government is expensive, and that we're unsatisfied with the result.

A brief look at your pay stub quickly shows exactly how much of our money the government takes—robbing us of the opportunity to use it to buy presents for our children, take dream vacations, or simply meet rent. But it's much harder to determine exactly how the government uses that (our) money to help us lead happier lives. While the cost of government taxation is crystal clear for most of us, the benefits are diffuse, usually invisible, and seemingly outside of our control. No wonder a sort of frustrated cynicism tends to descend on the American taxpayer, a cynicism that is all too easily transferred to our institutions as a whole, and our democratic processes in general.

What if American citizens had a direct role in how the government spends our tax dollars? This is the theory of Participatory Budgeting, a strategy for boosting citizen participation in democratic processes by allowing voters—the largest group of stakeholders—to influence how public dollars are spent. It turns out that offering constituents influence over the purse-strings of the state bolsters civic engagement across demographics and nationalities, increases citizens' understanding of governing processes, and makes participants more tolerant of differing political positions. In short, Participatory Budgeting helps build civic culture—that magical thing that happens when democratic dispositions are widely disbursed across a community of self-governors.

Participatory Budgeting (PB) practices appear to usher in civic culture for a simple reason: people feel that their participation will yield results. The budget will not double-talk or deceive them like an elected representative, which means the budget is something worth investing time into understanding and massaging. Candidates running for office and asking for your vote are adept at ducking such analysis with vague promises and duplicitous behavior. Participatory Budgeting, in short, is an extremely effective way to pull Americans into civic life. In endowing them with real responsibility, PB exhorts us all to develop the empathy for others, detailed understanding of our own interests, appreciation of trade-offs, and willingness to compromise that are necessary for enlightened democratic governance.

PARTICIPATORY BUDGETING IN K–12 SCHOOLS

As the institutions that most profoundly influences the behavior and worldview of America's youth, schools are uniquely positioned to teach students how collective governance works by involving them in decision-making processes. As school's most numerous and important stakeholder, and as the next generation of American self-governors, students have a powerful claim to power within school buildings.

Nothing engages young people in a task like involving them in it, and students who we expected to help lead our nation with integrity, intelligence, and grace as adults have no better training ground than schools, where they can wield meaningful power while surrounded by caring, capable adults who are trained in restraining and redirecting (inevitable, charming, and infuriating) youthful excesses.

There are many ways to offer young people some control over that first of their institutional relationships: the school. Here is a general template for starting a Participatory Budgeting program at your school.

ESSENTIAL ELEMENTS OF K–12 PARTICIPATORY BUDGETING

While PB programs vary widely across schools, all contain a few essential elements, which are:

1. School leadership that is willing to allocate some percentage of the school budget to student control. Generally, this is a small percentage (under 2 percent and often under 1 percent) in the context of the overall budget, but enough to implement (over $1,000 and ideally over $5,000) something new and meaningful to students

    a. If your school's budget does not allow PB, you can seek to raise money with the help of Parent Associations, local businesses, or good ole-fashioned grassroots fundraising.

2. A core group of student-leaders (between 3 and 25) who are committed to engaging their peers in school governance. These students might be elected by their peers into this leadership role or may be chosen by faculty and administrators.

    a. I call this core group of committed students the "Student Executive Board."

3. A faculty member or administrator committed to leading the Student Executive Board. This adult facilitator will help students choose their roles within the Executive Board and write the rules by which they will govern themselves.

Schools could run Participatory Budgeting as a class unto itself, infuse it into a social science elective, or found it as a school club.

Below is a step-by-step guide to starting a PB program at your middle or high school.

Step One: Present Participatory Budgeting to the School, then Recruit Student-Leaders

Present the premise and promise of Participatory Budgeting to your student body. Tell them how much money has been allocated for their use, outline the process by which they'll choose how it's spent, and ask excited students to join the Executive Board. Depending on timing and student interest, you can also hold elections to determine which students will sit on the Executive Board. Emphasize that the Executive Board will make its own operating procedures and have considerable latitude in determining how they govern themselves and the processes by which the student body as a whole will participate in the budgeting process. The Executive Board will act like elites in a democracy—setting the rules of participation for everyone else, while still being accountable to the ravages of public opinion.

Step Two: Executive Board Sets the Rules and Defines their Roles

Once the group of 3–25 students has been assembled, the faculty/admin leader asks them to develop their own rules of governance and define their roles against that of the student body at large. As America's great political philosophers would have advised, Participatory Budgeting works best when it's driven partially by direct democracy and partially by representative democracy. Here is one way to define roles:

Step 1

The PB Executive Board enumerates their responsibilities, which might include:

a. Developing ideas for how to use their money that the larger student body can vote on
b. Creating realistic budgets that reflect the types of projects that can be accomplished with the money allocated (e.g., rule out the possibility of building a new gym with $5,000)

   c. Maintain contact with relevant administrators as ideas are being discussed and parsed, to ensure that no idea goes outside the bounds of what the administration will allow

   d. Engage the larger student body in the process of idea generation, debate, and implementation

Step 2

The PB Executive Board puts out a "Call for Proposals" to the student body, asking students to submit ideas for how to spend the money. A subgroup of the Executive Board should be tasked with creating a thoughtful application and soliciting ideas throughout the application period.

Step 3

The PB Executive Board then winnows the submitted ideas down to those that are most feasible and meaningful. This should be done in consultation with relevant administrators.

Step 4

The PB Executive Board then presents the top ideas to the school and holds a final vote to determine the winning idea. *Rank choice voting* tends to work best when there are many ideas. If there are only 2–3 viable and compelling ideas, a simple winner-take-all voting system works well.

Step 5

Count the votes, announce the winner, then dissolve the PB Executive Board and choose an *Implementation Team* based on student interest. This team will lead the effort to ensure that the budget priority chosen by the student body is implemented in a timely manner. This may require working with administrators (and ensuring that they remain committed to the PB process), recruiting students to help in physical implementation (many schools choose to paint murals, add furniture or games to their gym, or otherwise physically alter their learning environment), and sharing progress with the school community as a whole (a sort of communications role).

   Participatory Budgeting gives students—any school's most important stakeholder—direct control over how the school looks, feels, and operates. Involving them in the budgeting process not only teaches them how to navigate the challenges of collective decision-making, the realities of institutional inertia, and the potential for skilled leaders to transform an environment, but it also endows them with the dignity of being a decision-maker. It makes them aware of their esteemed status in the school, the status of co-collaborators as well as charges. Co-collaborators feel the weight of the collective on their shoulders and feel compelled to invest their time into helping to build a healthy community. And when young people are invested in their schools—the first civic institution with which they build a relationship—the investment doesn't stop there. It transfers to an investment in their blocks, towns, cities, and nations.

Collective governance rests on a bedrock of shared habits, and schools incubate habits. By involving students to the operations of their schools, Participatory Budgeting teaches them how to advocate for their interests while respecting institutional norms. Democratic citizens must do the same.

Chapter Eight

Practicing Citizenship Strategy #2

Restorative Justice

When young people break rules and act like fools, they usually know what they're doing. Maybe they break rules because they don't fear consequences, maybe they're just trying to make a statement, and maybe they're simply moved by youthful impulse. Regardless, in breaking a rule, students express a lack of respect for the school community— they're telling those around them that their individual desires are more important than peace in the collective. In schools where rule-breaking is rampant and "trouble-making" kids are popular among their peers, adults in the school have lost control of school culture. Rather than imparting democratic values onto young people, disorderly schools allow the most bold and charismatic of their students to be the culture-creators. In the absence of meaningful direction from adults, the untrained minds of the young reign.

In general, there are two schools of thought on the topic of school discipline. One is trumpeted by high-performing charter school networks and can be summed up as "sweating the small stuff." Proponents of the "sweating the small stuff" style of discipline observe that disorderly schools fail at all of their goals: they can't teach young people math, English, social studies, or science, art, or philosophy if students refuse to stay in their chairs and pay attention, or if they're thinking about their next fight in the hallway. Since priority #1 for any school must be order, teachers and administrators are obligated to create a safe and predictable environment for the young people in the building. As any student of political science knows, order underlies nearly all forms of human progress. It precedes excellence and is a prerequisite for learning.

Therefore, student misbehavior must be dealt with swiftly and reliably from on high. Every teacher should treat every infraction in the exact same way, and students should be continuously reminded of what is expected of them by administrators and teachers. There should be no tolerance for students who question the disciplinary system, and there should be clear procedures in place for defiant students who refuse to submit to punishments.

In Robert Pondiscio's excellent book, *How the Other Half Learns*, which analyzes the strategies of the remarkable charter school network Success Academy, founder Eva Moskowitz quipped that when a student punches another student, the two students shouldn't be forced to participate in a discussion circle to talk through their feelings. The student who punched should be disciplined, and everyone else should move on. Her point is straightforward and compelling: students are in school to learn the content of each course, and school discipline should facilitate academic learning. Period. That means that discipline should be administered swiftly and uniformly. Asking students to participate in the disciplinary process distracts them from academics, which is the purpose of school.

But this book argues that schools must do more than teach academics. They must also mold young people into democratic citizens, and that takes more than merely imparting knowledge. It means shaping habits and involving them in school discipline is a powerful way of teaching the set of habits that enable collective governance. A disciplinary system that empowers students to render judgment on one another invites them into the school community like little else can. What better way to teach young people the responsibilities of self-government than to give them the reins over an institution's most oppressive power, the power to punish?

Restorative Justice practices—the second school of thought on school discipline—involve students in the disciplinary processes of the school. I argue that the habits that students develop when asked to balance order with individual freedom and the rights of their peers with the goals of the school are worth spending time on.

Clearly, school leaders can't simply hand over their disciplinary systems to students. Just as citizens in the United States participate in law-making within the liberal democratic framework erected by the US Constitution and Declaration of Independence, schools first instruct students in the school's core disciplinary principles, and then invite them to help implement and interpret those principles on a case-by-case basis.

Here are some ways to integrate restorative justice practices into school discipline without jeopardizing any school's first priorities of order and efficiency.

STRATEGIES FOR IMPLEMENTING RESTORATIVE JUSTICE PRACTICES INTO SCHOOL DISCIPLINE

Student Juries

Juries are one of our nation's most powerful democratic institutions, and one of its most resented. Few appreciate the experience of serving on a jury, and most do what they can to avoid it. Rather than an opportunity to serve, Americans tend to see jury duty as an annoyance, the avoidance of which justifies nearly all forms of low-level deceit.

But the opportunity to serve on a jury is a fundamental democratic check on a court system that is otherwise dominated by learned specialists with little accountability to the wider public. Jury duty should be seen as an honor, instead it's nearly universally regarded as a burden. Schools can change the culture around jury duty by requiring students to serve as jurors for their peers, a role that will be both educational and functional: functional because they will be given real input over the outcome of disciplinary cases, legitimizing the disciplinary process in the eyes of students and balancing out administrator and faculty biases, educational because faculty and administrators will explain the importance of a student jury for ensuring a truly just school disciplinary system.

Once students experience how juries can counterbalance institutional, elite biases in the justice system (in the admin and faculty in a school and in judges in a courtroom), they'll be proud of their service. Requiring young people to serve as jurors in their school community will give them a sense of the importance of juries in free, egalitarian societies. As adults, their attitudes toward jury duty may be a mixture of annoyance and pride rather than a pure distillation of the former.

Practical Considerations for Mandatory Student Juries

- Juries should be selected through a lottery system in the beginning of the year. Rather than waiting for a student disciplinary hearing to assemble a jury, juries should be pre-selected before any disciplinary hearings are scheduled.
- Once a hearing is scheduled, students with obvious biases (for example, if they're friends with the accused) should be reassigned to a different jury.
- Not every disciplinary hearing should include a jury—the school should internally decide which types of infractions call on a jury of peers.
- Student juries need not have formal powers. Depending on the culture and student-body of the school, this may be unwise, as young people are still developing their understanding of justice. Schools could allow jurors to decide the outcome of cases only if they reach a unanimous verdict. At a minimum, jurors should be required to offer their opinions of the case in writing and/or verbally either before or after a decision has been rendered.

Student Disciplinary Boards

Unlike Juries, Student Disciplinary Boards should have rigorous membership requirements and formal power. They should be composed of students who are recognized as even-tempered, fair-minded, and not subject to flattery or manipulation—from the administration or their peers. This should be a group of 3–11 who are nominated by a combination of faculty and students (perhaps members of the student government), serve for a set term, regularly meet to consider cases, and share authority with administrators.

Of course, the administration must have ultimate power—but by offering the Student Disciplinary Board some formal authority to check them or at least force them to listen to a young person's perspective, administrators build student capacity for considering fundamental questions of justice and articulating and defending moral positions. If young people are made a part of the creation and administration of disciplinary codes, they'll follow and defend those codes and exhort their peers to do the same.

While the precise powers and makeup of the Student Disciplinary Board should depend on the specifics of every school, a few general rules apply across contexts:

First, the Board should be nominated by students (probably by elected members of the student government) and confirmed by a subset of the school faculty. This arrangement reflects how state and federal justices are chosen—nominated by one set of officials (governors and presidents) and confirmed by another set (members of the legislative branch). While members of the faculty are of course unelected, requiring their sign-off on all members of the Student Disciplinary Board means that these members have won the trust of the entire school community.

Whoever introduces the Student Disciplinary Board to the school should not miss the opportunity to lead a discussion on the question of why these judicial positions are unelected—why shouldn't every position of power in a school (or nation) be an elected one? Students should also be asked to consider how the makeup of their school government reflects the makeup of the US government.

Discussion Circles

For fights, intense bullying, coordinated cheating, and other major betrayals of the school community, students should be made to verbally reflect on their behavior and explain their actions to a select group of adults. Adults who participate in discussion circles should project sincere curiosity and question students with goodwill and a desire to better understand why they did what they did. An accusatory tone will likely drive students into moody, defensive silence, and the goals of discussion circles is shared understanding and relationship-building.

Potential punishments should be discussed openly with students, and they should be able to offer their opinions on the most fitting punishment. Of course, the ultimate decision on their punishment will not be in their hands, but the opportunity to engage in dialogue with the adults who will help them understand why adults make the decisions that they do, and how exactly their behavior undermines school culture and harms those around them. Discussion circles are opportunities for administrators to talk through—rather than simply dictate—the logic of the school's disciplinary philosophy.

This will offer students who likely feel alienated from school administrators and who have opted out of the collective morality of the school community a peek under the hood of the disciplinary system. When young people are included in decision-making processes—even if the decision is to punish them—they buy into the school culture and community, because they at least understand how it works and why it does what it does. Including the most egregious offenders in their own disciplinary processes is dignifying, and young people respond to the signals of respect that inclusion endows.

Chapter Nine

Practicing Citizenship Strategy #3

*Student Governments that Build
School-Wide Civic Culture*

Student governments are a young person's first opportunity to participate in institutional leadership. As such, they should reflect the democratic institutions that students will grow up navigating as adults. Student body presidents and class presidents should be made to share
powers, and class representatives should be able to check both—teaching students that democratic governing bodies will be representative
before being efficient, and driving home the essential point that compromise is essential to a functioning democracy. Moreover, Student
Disciplinary Boards should function like the judicial branch of the US
government—insulated from the pressures of the student body, they
can render judgment without fear of retribution at the ballot box.

Student governments should also offer meaningful opportunities to
influence the day-to-day operations of the school. Rather than merely
executing directives from on high, student government representatives
should be able to meet with administrators and teachers on policy questions as a matter of course. If student governments lack real power,
they'll unwittingly send the message that popular governing is a cha-
rade (as it often is in other nations), and might dissuade young people
from participating in our government for the rest of their lives.

Finally, students should have the opportunity to contribute to the
collective governance of a school without holding a yearlong formal

title like "Class Representative" or "Student Body President." If student governments are to pull the student body as a whole into its sphere of engagement—thereby boosting school-wide civic culture—then there needs to be more opportunities for input and participation outside of elections and time-intensive, yearlong leadership roles. If student government is to serve as instruction for anyone outside of the already engaged and overachieving class of students, it needs to invite frequent participation from every type of student.

Opportunities for participation need to be bite-sized and customizable, so that every young person in the building can contribute in some way. There's no reason that student governments should be dominated by a small group of especially talented and hardworking youngsters. Self-governing communities need universal participation, and that means every young person must practice democratic governance in school. After all, in the near future everyone will be able to influence American politics—that means everyone needs to practice.

STUDENT GOVERNMENT STRUCTURE: STRUCTURES THAT MIRROR THE NATION AND SERVE THE SCHOOL

Student governments should be deeply integrated into the functioning of schools. Rather than silos of overachieving students who decorate hallways and carry out administrative orders, they should be bodies with meaningful authority and important responsibilities. Student influence should extend from the disciplinary system to the school budget, and members of the student government should be in regular dialogue with each other and administrators.

When a significant portion of the student body is engaged in the governance of their school, the culture of the school changes. The stereotypical teenage culture of cynical indifference to school rules and processes might give way to a culture that prizes thoughtful contribution to the school community.

Chapter Ten

Practicing Citizenship Strategy #4

*Student Referenda and Direct Proposals to
Faculty and Administration*

High school students should have the ability to propose changes in school policy directly to school decision-makers via a formal referenda-style process. Processes that allow any student—regardless of whether they're members of the Student Government or another student-governing body—to influence the school's operations can have a powerful effect on students' interest and engagement in the school community. Such a structure tells students that their input matters and invites them to share their voices as decisions are made.

A process that affords every student the opportunity to share their ideas directly with school administrators is a powerful antidote to the cynical indifference that can so easily define a teenager's relationship to their school. If they find a policy oppressive, wrong, or unfair, they can no longer use that policy to justify a lazy disdain for the school. It's up to them to change it.

The most effective systems that enable direct input from any student are two tiered. First, the student seeking a change in school policy must write down their proposed change in clear language and gather a minimum of 20 percent of their peers' signatures (larger schools might require a number rather than percentage, say fifty or a hundred student signatures) and the endorsement of one member of the faculty or administration. Students who succeed in this first step have demonstrated that their proposed change is popular across school stakeholders and have taken the time to build support for their proposal.

Next, the student author(s) of the proposal schedule a time to present their idea to the full faculty and administration, justifying the change, addressing concerns from their audience, and offering an implementation plan that accounts for logistical hurdles. After the presentation, the faculty and administration vote on whether to adopt the proposal. Generally, the faculty and administration must unanimously agree to support the proposal for it to go into effect. Some schools build in time to hear student presentations into their faculty meetings, and some hold monthly meetings focused exclusively on student proposals.

At the middle and elementary school levels, a similar process could take place within the context of a classroom. At the beginning of the year, when the teacher is presenting their class rules to their new class, students could be asked to propose a new class rule. Or they might be asked to do so in the middle of the year, once they've had the opportunity to function within the rules laid down by the teacher.

Even more simply, teachers could ask students to justify the class rules for themselves—explaining why each rule is important and why rules in general help us all succeed. Within that same activity, students could also be told to ask a question of one of the rules. Which rule do they not understand very well? Which of the rules seems unnecessary to them? This activity both forces young people to reflect on what it means for something to be "fair" and offers teachers an opportunity to fully explain why *their* rules *are* fair. Most importantly, it gets our very young people in the habit of analyzing and contributing to the rules that structure their lives, establishing in them the mindset of social contributor. As they get older, they'll see that our society at large also asks them to contribute to our shared rules, and that it's their duty and honor to do so with empathy and thoughtfulness.

Chapter Eleven

Practicing Citizenship Strategy #5

In-School Service Hours

To incentivize student participation on juries, disciplinary boards, student government bodies, and participatory budgeting projects, schools should strongly consider bifurcating their service hour requirements into "in-school service" and "out of school service." Currently, most high schools and many middle schools require students to complete a certain number of service hours to graduate (I've seen the number range from 10–25 hours per year). While this requirement does help local nonprofits and charities put on food drives, fundraising walks, and other large community events, the social impact of student service outside of school is mixed at best, and often negligible.

Generally, a young person will complete their hours by patching together various park cleanups, food drives, and other one-off events that are easy to find and require no ongoing commitment. By requiring students to serve in school as well as outside of it, administrators can more directly guide young people to opportunities that fit their talents and interests, coach them through the challenges that will inevitably arise, and push them to lead an institution that directly influences their daily lives. The truth is that most young people volunteer with organizations that mean little to them, in one-off ways that give them no sense of larger purpose.

They'd be loath to admit it, but most teenagers care about their schools and feel good when they do right by them. Everyone benefits when students step up their influence over more aspects of their schools and learn to balance their desires with those of the faculty, their parents, and the larger community.

Has a student had disciplinary issues in the past? They might be an excellent candidate to participate in the student disciplinary committee. Is a student underwhelmed by elective classes offered by the school? They might join the participatory budgeting committee, and push to hire a part-time teacher capable of teaching technology or art classes that currently don't exist. By pushing students to engage in in-school service and offering them a diverse menu of opportunities to contribute, schools force young people into the position of contributing to the collective as one of many governors. It's a position they'll be in from the time they're eighteen until they die. And it's one they'd do well to practice, lest they enter adulthood without this aspect of their identities—the understanding of themselves as citizens—developed.

Conclusion

"All education is moral education, because learning conditions conduct." —George Will, *Statecraft as Soulcraft*

Schools are not the sole cause of our fraught political climate, but they are our best hope for reform. Schools, with their ubiquitous presence in American life, have the power to shape the next generation's habits. They have the unique capacity to reward some types of behavior and discourage others, and it's in this capacity that they are best poised to help young people mature into logical, magnanimous, discerning, and engaged democratic citizens who understand, respect, and *live* American values. I've argued that schools' urgent mandate must be to structure their classrooms, homerooms, disciplinary processes, and lesson plans in ways that offer young people opportunities to *practice* the messy and frustrating work of democratic citizenship.

To teach collective deliberation, students should be asked to consider, assess, and weigh in on classroom and school-wide rules (and older students should be pushed to contribute to school rules as frequently as possible). Students must learn that both justice and excellence hinge on open and rigorous debate, and that the ability to express fact-based opinions and listen attentively to the concerns of others is at the heart of what it means to live in a democracy and to be an American. Finally, young people must recognize that the genius of democratic government is its capacity for people-driven renewal, and that disagreements among co-equal citizens is not only natural in a democracy but also essential to it.

Most importantly, this book seeks to persuade civics educators that our most important task is to convince young people to identify with the American values of open debate, people-driven renewal, and collective leadership. Civics education's most important mandate is to attach young people to values that define our nation, so that they identify as Americans before partisans, and can see clearly how partisan impulses undermine the national project. We are, of course, all entitled to our own worldviews, but free societies that enable the robust differences of opinion that we see today require a collective commitment to open, fact-based debate and consistent, widespread participation in public life. If we don't commit to those things first, we risk losing the free society that enables debate about everything else.

National culture runs through schools. As such, educators have an opportunity to orient future generations toward a more optimistic view of the American experiment, one that puts them—and their beliefs—at its center.

In a nation defined by its size and diversity, it's our values that hold us together and allow us to function as one, values that turn our differences from threats to our national cohesion into potent forces for national renewal. Since the American "we" is grounded in our values rather than shared ethnicity and ancient histories, that "we" must be cultivated in classrooms. The job of attaching young people to the principles of rigorous and peaceful debate, inclusive decision-making, and shared leadership—the task, in other words, of building a citizenry that is something more than a constellation of hostile factions—falls on our nations civics educators.

References

Allen, Danielle, Heinz, Stephen B., Liu, Eric P. *Our Common Purpose: Reinventing American Democracy for the 21st Century.* Cambridge, MA: The American Academy of Arts and Sciences, 2020.

de Tocqueville, Alexis. *Democracy in America.* London: Saunders and Otley, 1835.

Dewey, John. *Democracy and Education.* New York: Macmillan Publishers, 1916.

Gilman, Hollie Russon. *Engaging Citizens: Participatory Budgeting and the Inclusive Governance Movement within the United States.* Cambridge, MA: Harvard University, 2016.

Haidt, Jonathan. *The Righteous Mind: Why Good People Are Divided by Politics and Religion.* New York: Penguin Books, 2012.

Levitsky, Steven, Ziblatt, Daniel. *How Democracies Die.* New York: Penguin Random House, 2018.

Petrelli, Michael J. and Finn, Chester E. *How to Educate an American: The Conservative Vision for Tomorrow's Schools.* West Conshohocken, PA: Templeton Press, 2020.

Pondiscio, Robert. *How the Other Half Learns.* New York: Penguin Random House, 2019.

Putnam, Robert and Garrett, Shaylyn Romney. *The Upswing: How America Came Together a Century Ago and How We Can Do It Again.* New York: Simon and Schuster, 2020.

Putnam, Robert. *Bowling Alone: The Collapse and Revival of American Community.* New York: Simon and Schuster, 2000.

Ricks, Thomas E. *First Principles.* New York: HarperCollins, 2020.

Wallace, David Foster. *Consider the Lobster.* Boston, MA: Little Brown and Company, 2005.

Watkins, M. and Shulman, H. *Towards Psychologies of Liberation (Critical Theory and Practice in Psychology and the Human Sciences).* New York: Palgrave Macmillan, 2008.

Will, George. *Statecraft as Soulcraft: What Government Does.* New York: Simon and Schuster, 1984.

Zakaria, Fareed. *The Future of Freedom.* New York: W.W. Norton and Company, 2003.

About the Author

Andrew Tripodo designs social studies curricula for charter school networks, traditional public schools, and independent schools around the world. He is the cofounder of the educational nonprofit Knowledge of Careers, and a social studies teacher and director of the Society And Me Program at the Cushman High School in Miami, Florida.

He strongly believes that well-designed and delivered civics courses can inspire individuals and transform communities.

www.ingramcontent.com/pod-product-compliance
Lightning Source LLC
Chambersburg PA
CBHW020357270326

41926CB00007B/471